FIRST
GARDEN

How to Get Started in

Southern Gardening

■

Nellie Neal

with Rob Proctor

FIRST GARDEN

How to Get Started in

Southern Gardening

Nellie Neal

with Rob Proctor

Cool Springs Press

Nashville, Tennessee

Published by Cool Springs Press,
a Division of Thomas Nelson, Inc.,
P. O. Box 141000, Nashville, Tennessee 37214.

Library of Congress Cataloging-in-Publication Data
Neal, Nellie.
  How to get started in southern gardening / Nellie Neal, with Rob Proctor.
      p. cm. — (First garden)
  Includes index.
  ISBN 1-59186-161-6
  1. Gardening—Southern States. 2. Plants, Ornamental—Southern States. I. Proctor, Rob. II. Title. III. Series.
  SB453.2.S66N33 2005
  635.9'0975--dc22

                                                        2004030933

Printed in the United States of America
10 9 8 7 6 5 4 3 2 1

Book Development & Project Management: Marlene Blessing, Marlene Blessing Editorial
Copyediting: Melanie Stafford
Design & Formatting: Constance Bollen, cb graphics
First Garden Series Consultant: Darrell Trout
Map: Bill Kersey, Kersey Graphics

FRONT COVER: Images clockwise from upper left corner are pansy (JP), allium (JP), coleus (JP), and snowflake (TE). All photographs are copyright © Jerry Pavia (JP) and Tom Eltzroth (TE) as noted.

BACK COVER: A mix of spider flowers, salvia, and pink dahlias. Photograph copyright © Rob Proctor.

Cool Springs Press books may be purchased in bulk
for educational, business, fundraising, or sales promotional use.
For information, please email SpecialMarkets@ThomasNelson.com.

Visit the Thomas Nelson Web site at www.ThomasNelson.com
and the Cool Springs Press Web site at www.coolspringspress.net.

To Mary Trousdale Dunn,

who taught me to write

and to love begonias, to play canasta,

and to meet deadlines.

To my grandfather, 'Daddy' Tom Evans,

who showed me that digging in the dirt

is the most fun a person can legally have in this life.

His last garden on Earth was my first.

ACKNOWLEDGMENTS

No writer works entirely alone, and the creation of this book was no exception. Many thanks to two amazing gardeners and cherished friends whose brains I gladly pick every time we meet, Lily Singer and June Stevens. And to Melanie Dobel, for sharing her key to stress-free gardening.

Sincere thanks to fellow GWA members Linda Askey and Darrell Trout for essential networking on this project; you are the epitome of our profession.

Very special thanks to Marlene Blessing, Ringmaster of the First Garden books, for the gifts of benign neglect and gold stars.

FIRST GARDEN

SOUTHERN GARDENING

SECTION 2 / 65

Your Southern Garden
by Nellie Neal

PHOTOGRAPHY CREDITS

William Adams: 150

Liz Ball: 65 lower right, 96, 99 bottom, 149 top

Conard-Pyle Company/Star® Roses: 135 top

Mike Dirr: 106 top and bottom

Tom Eltzroth: 5, 15 upper left, 15 upper right, 15 lower right, 65 upper left, 66, 91, 103 top, 110 bottom, 114, 117 bottom, 120 bottom, 127, 128, 131 top, 135 bottom, 137, 138, 140 bottom, 142, 147, 149 bottom, 153 top, 156 bottom, 159

Dency Kane: 144 bottom

Charles Mann: 2, 110 top

Nellie Neal: 131 bottom

Jerry Pavia: 6, 15 lower left, 65 upper right, 65 lower left, 95 bottom, 109, 117 top, 123, 124 bottom, 132, 140 top

Rob Proctor: 16, 17, 18, 21, 24, 25, 27, 29, 30, 31, 33 upper left and 33 upper right, 34, 35, 37, 38, 40, 42, 44, 45, 48, 49, 51, 57, 59, 63, 66, 67, 69, 70, 71, 74, 77, 78, 80 left and right, 81, 82, 83, 84, 86 left and right, 89, 93, 95 top, 99 top, 100, 105, 119, 153 bottom, 160, 165

Felder Rushing: 103 bottom, 113, 120 top, 124 top, 144 top, 154, 156 top

For First-Time Gardeners Everywhere

No matter what part of the country you live in, it is possible to create a vibrant garden that adds beauty to your home and to your *life*. The First Garden series of books are meant for anyone who is just beginning to create his or her first garden. To someone who is new to gardening, a successful, thriving garden may seem like a feat to which only professionals and those with green thumbs can aspire. However, with a clear introduction to the basics—understanding your region (climate, soil, and topography); knowing the plants that grow best in your region; applying good design principles; and learning how to maintain and boost your garden's performance—you will quickly be able to start a garden. And do so with confidence! Before you know it, you may be sharing your garden dos and don'ts with your neighbor across the way.

In Section One of the book, you'll find easy-to-understand guidance to help you master the basics. As you read through this general introduction to gardening, written by nationally recognized garden expert Rob Proctor, you'll see photographs that aren't necessarily specific to your region. These are used to illustrate a design principle, technique, planting combination, or other important concept. Don't worry that your region has been forgotten! The entire final portion of the book, Section Two, is exclusively devoted to gardening specifics for your home turf. In addition to learning such things as how to improve your soil, when to plant bulbs, how to prune a tree or bush, and what kind of troubleshooting you may need to do, you'll also get a complete list of 50 sure-fire plants for your garden. Our regional garden experts have carefully selected these plants to enable you to have the best start possible as you begin what we hope will become a lifetime activity for you.

Like most pursuits, gardening takes time and patience to master. The First Garden books are designed to give you a reliable, can't-miss start. In addition to learning how to grow plants in your region, you will discover the process of turning your landscape into a beautiful, nurturing extension of your home. Even if you are beginning with only a few containers of plants on your deck or patio, you'll soon find that gardening rewards you with colors and scents that make your environment infinitely more satisfying.

With this book as your portable "garden expert," you can begin a great new adventure, knowing that you have friendly, clear advice that will keep you on the garden path. Most of all, we want to welcome you to gardening!

The Editors at Cool Springs Press

USDA Cold Hardiness Zone Map

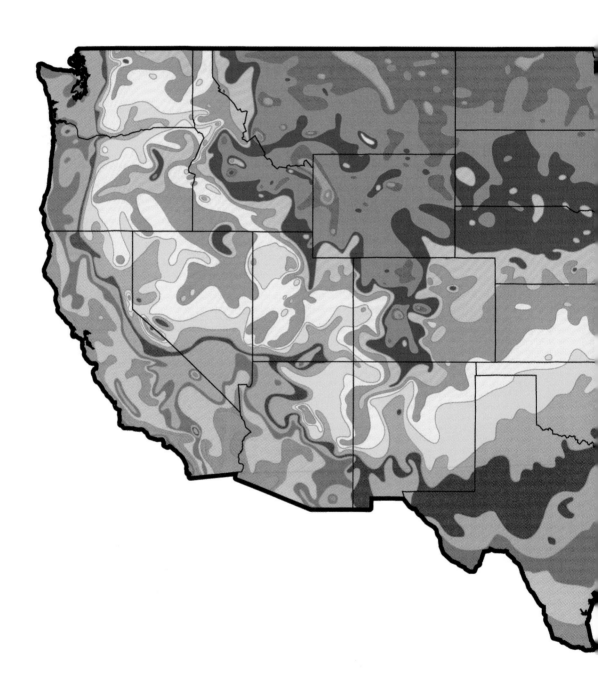

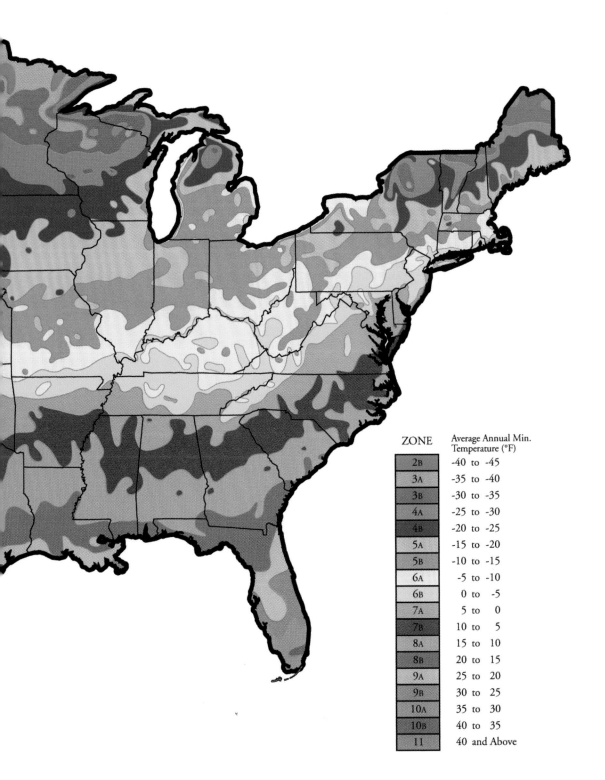

ZONE	Average Annual Min. Temperature (°F)		
2B	-40	to	-45
3A	-35	to	-40
3B	-30	to	-35
4A	-25	to	-30
4B	-20	to	-25
5A	-15	to	-20
5B	-10	to	-15
6A	-5	to	-10
6B	0	to	-5
7A	5	to	0
7B	10	to	5
8A	15	to	10
8B	20	to	15
9A	25	to	20
9B	30	to	25
10A	35	to	30
10B	40	to	35
11	40 and Above		

✿ Section 1

Your First Garden

Your first garden is unique. It might start as a blank canvas at a newly built house, without so much as a blade of grass. Or it could be an established landscape that you wish to make your own. Your approach will depend on your scenario. Your first garden might not even include land at the moment; perhaps, if you're an urban dweller, you've decided to garden on a rooftop or balcony.

Making a new garden is complex, intimidating, engrossing, and thrilling. It's all about color, design, and placement. Our visions dance before our eyes like sugar plum fairies. We're capable once again of that magic we used to know as children. My friend Wendy just started her first garden, and I helped her with some planning and took her shopping for plants. We filled her SUV and she rushed home to plant. She called me to say she was "enthralled in the madness" and some of our initial planning went out the window as her creative juices flowed. Good for her!

It would be rare if a garden turned out exactly as planned. However, countless TV makeover shows lead us to believe that this can happen. We see the plan, then some fast-motion digging and planting, then the finished project and the dazed surprise of the happy homeowner. This

---

Visions spring to life in the form of satiny Iceland poppies, coral bells, and tiny 'Zing Rose' dianthus

Lush and romantic, this garden features roses scrambling onto a wagon wheel, coral Jupiter's beard, spikes of fireweed, and a pink skirt of Mexican evening primrose.

---

all happens in the course of several days, boiled down to less than a 30-minute show. But then what? What happens to the new garden afterward?

Don't get me wrong. I like these shows and often get good design ideas from them. But without a follow-up, we don't have any idea what became of the transformation we've just witnessed. Did the owner water enough? Too much? Did the plants get enough sun? Did those vines cover the new trellis that hides that ugly garage wall? Did the perennials fill in like a soft carpet around the new pond? Or did bindweed and thistle sprout everywhere, choke out the new plants, and return the area to its former dilapidated, dismal state?

My own first garden was poorly planned, badly designed, chock-full of mistakes—and absolutely wonderful. Filled with boundless enthusiasm and unwarranted confidence from growing up in a gardening family, I blundered my way within a few years to creating a garden that was the subject of glamorous layouts in three magazines. In the process, I devoured hundreds of gardening books, subscribed to every horticultural magazine and newsletter I could find, visited every public and private garden I could, and lost twenty pounds.

I planted, transplanted, divided, amended, pruned, mulched, whacked, hacked, hoed, pinched, seeded, and fertilized until my thumb turned green. Making your first garden can be one of the most stimulating and creative experiences of your life. It might also be frustrating, confusing, and occasionally heartbreaking. It all depends on how you do it. You can take small steps or giant leaps. I'm a leaper myself, but I appreciate the cautious, practical approach, of which I'm incapable. The kind of people who plan meticulously might need a big sketch pad and several notebooks (you're probably mentally planning a shopping trip for this purpose at exactly 4:45 P.M. tomorrow afternoon). And it wouldn't hurt to construct a storyboard (borrow the bulletin board from your kid's room) of pictures and articles clipped from magazines, photos from friends' and public gardens, and even key words you want to remember as overriding themes. "Romantic," "lush," "bountiful," and "low-maintenance" don't go in the same sentence, by the way. But we'll talk about realistic maintenance later.

> **My own first garden was poorly planned, badly designed, chock-full of mistakes— and absolutely wonderful.**

Your notebooks can start to fill with color swatches; plant "wish lists"; clippings from the paper; brochures from fence, irrigation, and patio furniture companies; and preliminary budget figures. This might sound a bit like decorating a living room (and indeed your garden will be a "living" room), but there's a difference. With an indoor space you actually reach a point where it's considered finished. With a garden—as an evolving place—it's never completely finished, just done "for now." A garden that doesn't change is not only impossible, but I guarantee you would find it boring.

■ Discovering Your Inner Gardener

When you begin to garden, there are so many considerations it's tough to know where to start. So let's start with you. Do you like gardening work? That means watering, fertilizing, digging, planting, pruning, and all that? Not to mention the dreaded "W" word—weeding. Unlike tennis or ballet, gardening doesn't require any particular talents or physical attributes such as grace or brute strength. It just takes industriousness. People who like to keep house or fix cars, for example, may make fine gardeners, because the plans of attack to get the job done are similar.

Gardening is the number-one pastime in our country. Perhaps not everyone practices it to a refined degree, but this does mean that, in general, we enjoy the pleasures of working in the soil and raising flowers and vegetables. Your garden is what you make it. You'll be surprised how quickly you'll pick up the knowledge and skills to make yours beautiful and productive. Gardening is part art and part science, so there's room for everybody—right- or left-brainers— to get into the act. A friend of mine once called gardening the "slowest of the performing arts." You're the director and the plants you grow are the stars and supporting players.

As the director of your horticultural extravaganza (as well as the set designer, head writer, and entire technical crew), start with your vision. Some people might begin with a low-budget home movie, and others envision an epic blockbuster. Our inspirations come from many sources— childhood memories, books and magazines, and travels. And since I've drawn an analogy to the movies, let's acknowledge that many of us find inspiration on the silver screen as well. Sometimes

I feel my garden resembles the one in *The Secret Garden*. Before the children cleaned it up. (By the way, those were remarkably skilled kids, outperforming a crew of at least 20 landscapers.)

■ Blueprints for the Garden

As you plan your garden and its "rooms," take a look at what you've got—at ground level and below. City and suburban dwellers often live in a house that sits on a square, flat lot. Even a rooftop or balcony gardener usually deals with a level rectangular space. On the other hand, perhaps you live amidst hills, valleys, embankments, or even streams or ponds on your property. Your nearest neighbor may be feet or miles away.

It's probably time to clarify the difference between a landscape and a garden. Although the two are connected, there are some differences. A landscape applies to everything on the property, but most specifically trees, shrubs, and hardscape (walkways, walls, driveways, decks, patios). A landscape may include "garden areas" as a part of its overall scheme. The traditional American landscape typically features a lot of lawn, "foundation plantings" of shrubs that hug the house, and various trees placed for shade. It's a nice, familiar picture, perhaps with a strip of geraniums or petunias bordering the walk. Or maybe there's a flowerbed skirting the row of junipers or yews lined up under the eaves of the house.

The footprint of your house, any outbuildings, and adjacent buildings define your site. One way or the other, you may wish to make a blueprint of your property to draw and dream upon. It doesn't need to be exactly to scale (or even blue). I wouldn't even recommend doing much detailed planning on it since one-dimensional blueprints rarely translate into beautiful three-dimensional gardens. Just use it to familiarize yourself with all the features of your existing site (or lack of them) and for the placement of present and future walkways, driveways, patios, walls, trees, and specific garden areas or features. These could be things such as herb, cutting, or vegetable gardens as well as borders, ponds, play areas, and so forth. I often sketch on a legal pad to help me plan or revamp an area. (I once designed a friend's garden on a cocktail napkin, but that's another story that taught me I need a bigger piece of paper.)

If you picture creating a garden that is more unique, you won't need to exclude any of these traditional elements. Instead, you'll treat them somewhat differently and focus more directly on flowers and vegetables and their relationships to everything else on the property. In this scenario, there's a nearly constant, hands-on relationship between you and the plants, far beyond a weekly mowing or annual hedge trimming. If you really like plants, you can transform any static landscape into an active garden.

■ About Soil

What color is your thumb? People who meet me often feel obliged to apologize for their black thumbs. "I kill everything," they tell me. There's no such thing as a black thumb. Everybody can garden. Plants—like pets—need water, food, a suitable place to live, and occasional grooming. Green thumbs aren't born, they're made. The origin of the term stems from the fact that gardeners put excessive wear and tear on their thumbs and forefingers. As they pinch petunias or pull pigweed, the green sap stains eventually become engrained for most of the gardening season. My thumb's not a classic green but more of a dirty olive tone. Let's not mention my knuckles and nails, which are accented by various cuts, scrapes, and punctures.

You don't need to ruin your hands. Sensible glove-wearing gardeners still deserve the title green thumb. You can earn it, too. Learn the basics and build on those, just the way you'd approach any new pastime such as cooking, tennis, sewing, or carpentry.

Okay, former black thumbs: get started. Dig a spadeful of soil. (If you're a rooftop or balcony gardener, skip this and go buy some potting soil.) Squeeze a handful. Does it stick together into a mud ball? You have clay. That's most of us. If the ball of soil falls apart, you've got sand. It's an easier soil to dig, but dries out more quickly. If you're extremely lucky, you're blessed with rich, black "Iowa cornfield" soil that gardeners crave (in which case you're probably reading this in Iowa). Don't worry. Both clay and sandy soil can be amended to grow some traditional plants. On the other hand, a good many plants are so adaptable that they'll grow well in almost any kind of soil.

Once you've done some experimenting, you can decide what—if anything—you want to do to your soil. I actually don't amend soil, but grow what wants to grow in that soil. I've often read or seen experts who recommend a soil test. I've never done one. I wouldn't have a clue what it meant if I had 100 parts magnesium

> **Green thumbs aren't born, they're made.**

A garden planted in unimproved clay soil, rarely irrigated, supports many drought-tolerant perennials including varieties of penstemons and bright Jupiter's beard.

per million. Unless you suspect that your soil has an actual problem (such as being missing after the builders finished the house) or has some sort of contamination, I can't imagine the value of a test unless you want to grow rare alpine plants from Switzerland. Even if your soil has been pounded and pulverized by heavy equipment, you don't need a soil test to tell you it's been compacted and that with just a little more pressure will turn into diamonds. Most people have the kind of soil that everybody else in their neighborhood has. What's growing there? Does it look healthy? If the trees are dying and lawns are sickly, don't get a soil test—call the Environmental Protection Agency.

Your soil will actually teach you as you go along what it's capable of doing. It may not support absolutely every type of plant you might want to grow (I'll never have blueberries), but odds are it has plenty of potential. For extreme sand or clay, you may decide to amend or alter your soil or bring in topsoil for plants with specific needs (I would need to create an acidic bog to grow blueberries). But first explore what your soil can do before you begin a wholesale radical makeover that will forever alter its composition.

Don't just start adding ingredients willy-nilly. Many books often recommend adding lime to the soil as a matter of course. The assumption is that most plants do best if grown in a soil that is about neutral on the pH scale. This advice may be all well and good in Cleveland or Boston where the soil pH is on the acid side, for the lime would reduce the acidity. But for gardeners in the West, which generally has an alkaline soil, the lime would be a waste of time, like giving "The Rock" a gym membership for his birthday. The point is to be familiar with your soil type and composition, but don't stress about it.

■ Weather and Gardening Zones

Before you start thinking about planting, determine in which climate zone you live. The U.S. Department of Agriculture (USDA) issues a detailed map, found at the front of this book, that illustrates these zones throughout the country. Based primarily on average minimum temperatures, the map helps you determine which plants will survive in your area. Almost all the plants you buy will be rated as to the zones where they are hardy, meaning where they'll survive an average winter. Most nurseries in your region only carry plants that are appropriate to it. But if you purchase plants online or by mail, you should be aware of your zone so you don't end up planting a tropical palm in Minnesota.

> Many gardeners expand their options by clever gardening known as "zone denial."

IN THE ZONE

The USDA climate zone map is a good aid in helping you decide what to grow, but it has its limitations. For example, it doesn't take into account rainfall, humidity, and, most importantly, high temperatures. These factors also affect plant survival. You'll find that Chicago, Denver, and Hartford are all categorized as zone 5, but their actual growing conditions vary considerably. Rainfall, humidity, and summer heat—as well as soil type—may play as great a role in plant performance as winter low temperatures. Southern gardeners sometimes find that plants considered hardy for their zone won't thrive in their summer heat or need a colder winter dormancy than southern climes provide. Tulips are a case in point. It all sounds terribly complicated, but as you visit local nurseries and gardens, you'll get the hang of it. You'll soon start to get a grasp of what wants to grow in your area.

MICROCLIMATES

Adhering to the zone designations may help you play it safe, but many gardeners expand their options by clever gardening known as "zone denial." After all, plants can't read. If they receive the conditions that allow them to thrive, they will. This is where knowing your garden site intimately is vital. Throughout it there are "microclimates," little pockets formed by topography, fences, trees, and walls. Your house offers the most differentiations. Southern and western exposures are usually hotter and sunnier; northern and eastern exposures, cooler and shadier. The placement of trees can moderate or enhance these conditions.

A hill or outcropping may afford at least two distinct microclimates in much the same way as your house does. Lower areas tend to be cooler and, because cold air sinks, often freeze earlier than higher ground, as well as collecting and holding moisture. Knowing this helps you to position plants that prefer either well-drained soil (on a slope) or moist soil (in a hog wallow). Both air and water drain in the same manner on a large scale. Cold air often "flows" along streams and rivers, making low-lying areas "frost pockets" and higher ground "banana belts." If you're in a low-lying area, there's not much you can do about this, of course, except to be more cautious about setting out tender plants in spring or protecting them in the fall. If you're on a hilltop, you can just feel smug. But hilltops may get fierce winds (in gardening, there's a plus and minus to every condition). Knowing the direction of the prevailing wind helps prevent mistakes as well; otherwise you may be staking your delphiniums with rebar.

Paving and foundations, as well as rocks and rock outcrops also affect plant performance, either for better or worse, depending on the plant. Some plants revel in the extra heat from driveways, walkways, and foundations, and others can't stand baking. Many plants also like to get their roots beneath rocks and paving not only because of the extra heat, but because the mass of the stone moderates the surrounding temperatures by virtue of its slow heating and cooling. Rock gardeners exploit these possibilities to the max, with every nook and cranny offering a potential microclimate for a special plant.

Wherever you live, you can create a beautiful garden. Gardeners often envy others who live in different climates, usually because of particular plants that grow beautifully in that environment. By all means, experiment to see if you can achieve similar results. But don't get hung up on a certain flower that has little intention of performing for you. Yes, I've made attempts to grow azaleas and rhododendrons that I admire in friends' gardens in Virginia. And failed. So I'm content to visit them in spring and enjoy their good fortune. They come to see me, too, to admire western specialties that their gardens can't accommodate successfully, like prickly poppies and penstemons.

Although we often equate an abundance of moisture with successful gardening, it's only because the spectacular gardens in rainy regions get most of the good press. Lovely, original gardens are found within every region of our country. They are filled with the plants that want to grow there. Some may be native wildflowers, and others may originate in areas around the

A rock-terraced slope provides good drainage and extra heat for purple verbena, agave, and ice plants, with a backdrop of golden black-eyed Susans.

world with similar climate and soil. Fortunately for all of us, there's an enormous pool of plants that offer amazing abilities to adapt to a wide spectrum of conditions. Like our country itself, your new garden is likely to become a melting pot of flowers and styles from many lands—with your very own personal stamp.

■ Plant Names: Why Latin?

There's no escaping it. You need a little Latin—not much, but a little. Every living thing, animal and plant, is classified scientifically using a system that speaks Latin. To keep the millions of distinct forms of life in some sort of reasonable order, they all have a scientific name, much like our first and last names. It avoids duplication. If you looked in the phone book under Mary Jones or Bob Smith, you understand how confusing it could get if we just called plants "bluebell" or "daisy."

Most people know more scientific plant names than they think. Even non-gardeners are familiar with *chrysanthemum, geranium, lobelia, dahlia, crocus, phlox, gardenia, verbena, begonia,* and *petunia.* Others aren't much of a stretch, such as *rosa* for rose, *lilium* for lily, *tulipa* for tulip, or *hyacinthus* for hyacinth.

Within any genus of plants or animals there are individual species. Let's start with people. We all belong to the genus *Homo,* meaning human. And our species is *sapiens,* meaning wise or intelligent. We belong to the classification "intelligent human." We don't need to draw this distinction very often since the rest of the members of our genus are extinct. *Homo erectus* was "standing man," who apparently could walk upright but wasn't known for his brain. The traits of particular plants are often noted in their species name, called the specific epitaph, such as their color, habit, size, leaf shape, their resemblance to something else, what habitat they grow in, their country or region of origin, or something like that. They don't always make a whole lot of sense. Sometimes they honor a botanist who first discovered them or somebody to whom the discoverer wanted to suck up. After all, who wouldn't want a plant named for them? Most plants were named hundreds of years ago, although new discoveries occasionally crop up in rain forests.

When plant breeders get involved, plants acquire yet another name. Say that you, as a plant breeder, cross two different species to create a brand-new offspring with distinctly different characteristics from the two parents. Or say that, as a sharp-eyed gardener or nursery owner, you spot an unusual variation in an otherwise uniform batch of plants. What do you do? Name it, of course, for your wife, husband, mother, daughter, or a celebrity you admire. Or if you're more creative, you go for something more lyrical or amusing. That's why we have *Anemone* x *hybrida* 'Honorine Jobert' (named for the guy's daughter), the hybrid tea rose 'Dolly Parton' (a voluptuous flower), and the self-descriptive petunia 'Purple Wave' (the color really flows). I've always hoped to create a new color of the trailing annual *Bacopa* and call it 'Cabana'. The gardening world is waiting. . . .

Penstemon fanciers need to know the scientific names of pink *Penstemon palmeri* and purple *P. strictus.*

> When it comes to pronunciation, don't stress. Latin is a dead language. It's nobody's native tongue. ❧

As for the scientific names, we don't use them very much except for perennials. Not too many people say *quercus* instead of oak or *curcubita* instead of squash (unless they're really, really snobbish). Whenever a common name will do, use it. Most gardeners—in my opinion—should just talk about daylilies, Russian sage, and yarrow without trying to tie their tongues around *hemerocallis, perovskia,* or *achillea.* But in some cases, especially when you're talking about a genus with a whole bunch of species, and you need to get specific about which one, the only way is to use Latin. There are hundreds of varieties of *penstemon,* for example. These lovely western wildflowers, commonly called beardtongue (yuck), range from tall scarlet *Penstemon barbatus* to mat-forming blue *Penstemon virens.* Then there's pretty orange *P. pinifolius,* lovely pink *P. palmeri,* and wispy white *P. ambiguas.* If you get into penstemons, you gotta speak the lingo.

When it comes to pronunciation, don't stress. Latin is a dead language. It's nobody's native tongue. Do your best with this cumbersome old language. And if someone dares to correct your pronunciation of a name, just stare him or her down coolly and say, "Oh, that's the way I used to say it." This implies that you have been hanging out with more knowledgeable gardeners than they have and you must obviously be right.

Sort out the easy mispronunciations before you go to the nursery so you don't have them snickering behind your back. *Cotoneaster* is "ka-tone-ee-aster" not "cotton Easter." I'd say flowering tobacco for *nicotiana,* but if you must, pronounce it "ni-coh-she-anna" not "nikko-teen-a." Avoid *aquilegia* ("ah-qui-lee-ja" not "a-quill-a-gee-a"), and just say columbine instead.

■ Plant Types

TREES: GARDEN ELDERS

All this talk of sites, soils, and climates brings us to the basic business of knowing and growing plants. Plants have evolved to fill niches created by geography and topography. Trees tower above everything (sort of like carnivores on the food chain). They're tough and long-lived. Any tree planted today will, with care, likely outlive any of us, so its placement is the most critical of any plant you put in the soil. Trees need space. With their specific needs varying by species, they need enough room between them and your house, each other, power lines, and features like that. In most cities, the office of forestry offers guidelines and regulations on tree planting. Street trees especially must be placed so as to not block sight lines at intersections or to interfere with power lines and street lights. If you get it wrong, some city employee will probably pay you a visit. Some kinds and types of trees are even forbidden because they are brittle and are prone to breaking under snow and ice or from wind, which endangers cars and passersby. Multistemmed trees such as redbuds or dogwoods are often prohibited for planting along streets since they can block the views at intersections. Most drivers can see around a single trunk tree adequately, but a big mass of foliage is dangerous.

Breaks in the canopy of trees allows beds of perennials and ornamental grasses to flourish in this well-conceived plan.

Trees differ in many ways. Evergreens hold their leaves (called needles if the tree is a spruce, pine, fir, or cypress) throughout the year, while deciduous trees drop their leaves in fall and grow new ones in spring. In frost-free climates, some trees hold their leaves throughout the year, while others still go through a seasonal renewal. At least two kinds of "evergreen" tree, the larch and bald cypress, go dormant in fall and drop their needles. There's an infamous tale in my city of a park maintenance crew who, thinking that it had died, cut down a prized bald cypress that was just in the bald phase of its normal cycle.

All trees flower. Some do it in spectacular fashion, while others are barely noticed except by allergy sufferers. Bees and other insects usually pollinate trees with big, showy, and scented flowers, such as fruit trees. Most other trees rely on the wind to blow about their massive amounts of pollen, which is precisely why spring can be so miserable for some of us.

Most trees have a single main trunk, and most deciduous trees create an interlocking canopy of branches. Trunks of every tree should always be respected and protected. While appearing to be the strongest part of the tree, the trunk is also the most vulnerable. Just beneath the bark is the lifeline of the tree, called the cambium layer, the vascular system that supports the tree the way our veins and arteries support us. When bark is damaged, that damage is usually irreversible, and the limbs on that side of the tree will often die. Even something as insignificant as a weed whacker can damage or kill a tree.

Tree roots need respect and protection, too. Compaction of the soil above the roots is to be avoided as this suffocates them and inhibits their ability to absorb water. The roots that do most of the work of searching for food and water, called feeder roots, are usually at and beyond the shady circle cast by the tree at high noon. This is called the drip line, because rain splashes from leaf to leaf, keeping the area directly beneath relatively dry. Remember that it doesn't do much good to water a tree right at the trunk since its feeder roots are many feet away.

WOODY PLANTS: SPACE AND CARE

Trees are durable because they're made of wood. This is either patently obvious or extremely profound, but I thought it needed to be said. Other woody plants—call them shrubs or bushes, it doesn't matter—are structured like trees. They can also be deciduous or evergreen, but their main similarity is their strong, woody constitution. All the considerations you give to a tree in placement and care apply to shrubs. One of the chronic mistakes that plague American gardeners is to crowd shrubs and not give them enough room to develop. This leads to much whacking and hacking, resulting in distorted, weird-looking bushes, often represented by the classic "light bulb" trim job. I know you've seen it. You've probably also driven past houses that have almost completely disappeared behind rampaging junipers whose growth habits the owners underestimated. There's a hilarious example in my neighborhood where the people neglected to read the tags when they planted cone-shaped junipers in front of their picture windows. Eventually, the view disappeared as the trees grew higher than the house. The owners then decided to trim all the branches below the roofline, leaving thick bare trunks with little "Christmas trees" perched upon them. I chuckle every time I drive by, but there's a lesson in that for all of us.

Most shrubs we grow in our gardens are either selected for their evergreen nature (often for winter interest) or for their flowers. A few, such as holly, are grown primarily for their handsome berries. Almost all flowering shrubs bloom on "old" wood, meaning only branches a year or more old will produce flowers. Keep in mind that if you do prune or trim (shrubs usually need much less grooming than we think), it should be done only right after they've finished blooming. Otherwise you'll be cutting off your next years' display.

ROSES: TENDER OR TOUGH

Roses are certainly the most popular of the shrubs. Novice gardeners want to grow them in the worst way. First-time rose growers envision huge bouquets of long-stemmed tea roses on their dining room tables. It's a nice dream, but those roses you received on Valentine's Day were greenhouse grown in supporting cages to keep their stems straight and long. And the bushes never experienced arctic winters or Saharan heat. Yours probably will.

Let's get realistic about roses. You'll have some for cutting, but don't get any ideas about opening your own flower shop. Wherever you garden, you can successfully grow hundreds of varieties of roses. Just don't get hung up on the hybrid teas at the beginning. Just as rewarding are the old-fashioned shrub roses, climbers, floribundas, and the so-called landscape roses and carpet roses. Most thrive with a minimum of care and some are even drought tolerant.

Shrub roses say romance in the garden. With their graceful, arching canes laden with sweet blooms, they conjure nostalgic visions of castles and cottages. Superb performers, they seldom, if ever, suffer from pests or diseases beyond an aphid or two (easily dispatched with a soapy spray). Widely grown across much of the nation are the classic early bloomers such as 'Persian

Yellow', 'Austrian Copper', and 'Harrison's Yellow'. The red-leaf rose, *Rosa glauca*, takes the prize as the most adaptable shrub rose. It will thrive in conditions from sun to part shade, clay to sand, and wet to dry. Pretty little single pink flowers grace the unusual leaves, blue-gray on top with maroon red underneath.

These large shrub roses can often be found in older neighborhoods where they put on spectacular early displays. Young shrub roses are like gawky teenagers, irregular and awkward looking. Give them space and time to fulfill their promise. Some people avoid planting these classics because they bloom only once each season. That's unfair. After all, I've never heard anyone complain because his or her lilacs, tulips, or lilies bloom only once a year.

Some shrub roses do bloom persistently, even in heat. The *rugosa* hybrids are simply wonderful. If I had to choose just one, it would be 'Therese Bugnet' (pronounced "boon-yay"). On bushes 4' by 5', its glossy green foliage supports full, pink flowers with the perfect "old rose" perfume. I'm also entranced by 'Golden Wings', an upright shrub type that grows to 4' or 5' tall. Its huge, single amber yellow flowers are accented by orange stamens and carry a soft fragrance. For an arbor or trellis, the classic ruby red 'Blaze' can't be beat, while pale pink 'New Dawn' is the stuff of fairy tales. Speaking of which, 'The Fairy' is a dainty but tough little shrub about 3' by 3' with nonstop clusters of satin pink blooms. It's beautiful with lavender or catmint as a "skirt" (most roses are lovely coupled with these plants). All these roses grow well in most regions, but there are certainly regional favorites that you can visit at local municipal gardens. Look

> **Wherever you garden, you can successfully grow hundreds of varieties of roses.**

Adobe-toned yarrow and a flurry of snow daisies enhance the much-admired classic hybrid tea rose 'Peace.'

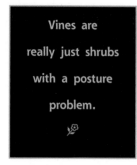

Vines are really just shrubs with a posture problem.

for ones that demonstrate unusual vigor and clean, disease-free leaves. Also keep in mind how much room you want to devote to each bush. Can you accommodate the big boys, or are you best with the little guys?

Other compact varieties that perform tirelessly are the Meidiland series in white, coral, reds, and pinks. Easy and prolific, their single or double flowers fit in effortlessly with perennials such as meadow sage, pincushion flowers, catmints, snow daisies, and yarrow. Most roses—to my mind—look their best planted informally rather than regimented in rows. Hybrid tea roses benefit enormously when surrounded by casual companions that enhance their charms and disguise their weaknesses. To keep the advice short and sweet: plant roses in sun, keep them evenly moist, feed regularly, and prune in spring. I'm fond of a number of hybrid tea roses, but my favorite is the elegant cream and pink 'Peace'. This classic rose, bred in France just before World War II, survived because its breeder shipped a single cutting to a friend in America just before the Nazis invaded. The rest of the roses were destroyed, but 'Peace' endured. Just one of its flowers, floating in a bowl, is all any rose lover needs.

VINES: BEAUTIFUL CLIMBERS

Vines are really just shrubs with a posture problem. They've found a special niche in nature where they rely on their neighbors for support. The ultimate in social climbers, they cling and twine their way to ever-greater heights. Since they are lovely, we forgive them and give them fences, arbors, and trellises on which to grow and flower. Some enchant us with their flowers—clematis, honeysuckle, and wisteria—and others with their foliage—ivy and Virginia creeper. Grapes mean jelly, juice, and wine, and hops are a vital ingredient in beer. I've never made homemade wine or beer, but both grapes and hops make beautiful, albeit rambunctious, additions to the garden. A few very popular vines, such as morning glories and sweet peas, grow, flower, and die in one season, which makes them annuals. We'll talk about them shortly.

A planting of roses and perennials, including pink lupines and white valerian, is peppered with annual bread seed poppies.

PERENNIALS: LASTING PLEASURES

Perennial plants have a completely different strategy for survival than trees and shrubs. When cold weather hits, they retreat underground and wait out winter with their root systems. They return "perennially" each spring. Don't confuse "perennial" with "immortal," however, as some

**Annuals in concert—glowing pink 'First Love' dianthus scores with
blue and white forms of mealy-cup sage.**

perennials run their course in just a few years. Others live to a very old age, such as peonies and daylilies. Since about the last quarter of the twentieth century, most Americans have based the bulk of their gardens around perennials. Just as hemlines go up and down and lapels go wide and then skinny, gardens go through periods of what's in and out. At the moment and for the foreseeable future, perennials figure prominently in most gardens. With trees and shrubs as the backdrop and structure of the garden, perennials take center stage. They're valued for their diversity, toughness, longevity, and—above all—beauty. A wonderful trend in American gardening today is to value every sort of plant and use it to best advantage. While Victorians didn't have much use for perennials, preferring showy, hothouse-raised annuals, we've come to embrace all kinds of plants regardless of their life cycles.

ANNUALS: COLORFUL ADDITIONS

When we picture annuals, we think of those vibrant, tempting flowers bursting out of their six-packs every spring at garden centers, supermarkets, and home improvement stores. These are the plants we rely on for continuous color all summer long. Usually grown from seed, annuals germinate, grow, flower, set seed, and die in a single season. It's a short, but dazzling life cycle. What's considered an annual depends on where you live. In most northern climates, the annual section includes many tender tropical and subtropical perennials, such as geraniums, that aren't hardy below freezing. My sister in Florida has geraniums older than her ancient cat. So in this category, we're including plants with a single-season life cycle in whichever climate you garden. Your local nursery can help you sort it all out. Many gardeners in cold-winter climates move these tender perennials indoors to save them from year to year.

Most annuals come packaged in handy six-packs or four-packs, but for the impatient, many garden centers offer mature blooming annuals in quart- or gallon-size pots. These, of course, come with higher price tags, but presumably are worth it for those who want instant gratification. A number of annuals aren't very suitable for six-packs, and grow best if sown directly in the ground. You'll save money as well as expand your selection if you learn to grow plants from seed. To build your confidence, start with the easy ones like sunflowers and marigolds.

Annuals prove themselves invaluable in a new garden because they grow to full size quickly. While everything else—trees, shrubs, and perennials—put down roots for the long haul, annuals fill the gaps and encourage the new gardener. But they're much more than gap-fillers. Even as the rest of the garden takes off, leave room for the gorgeous gaiety that annuals provide. I'd never want to go through a season without the brilliant blossoms of California poppies, moss roses, larkspurs, zinnias, or salvias. Annuals truly shine in container gardens as well. As mentioned previously, several vines are annual in nature. Among the most popular are morning glories, sweet peas, hyacinth beans, sweet potato vines, canary creepers, and climbing nasturtiums, not to mention peas and pole beans.

Many annuals that find your garden to their liking may respond by sowing themselves from year to year, making a one-time investment in them a very good one indeed. These "volunteers" can be thinned and transplanted to suit you. Johnny-jump-ups, larkspurs, bachelor's buttons, sweet alyssum, and several kinds of poppy—California, Shirley, corn, and lettuce-leaf—likely will form colonies in your garden. Count yourself lucky.

The care of annuals is as diverse as the plants themselves. Some like constant attention with lots of water and fertilizer. Some prefer benign neglect. Morning glories, cosmos, and nasturtiums—if fed and watered too much—will reward you with jungle-like growth, but deny you their flowers. It's called too much of a good thing.

BULBS: SPRING AND FALL

Bulbs take their preservation to extremes. Spring-flowering bulbs such as tulips and daffodils bide their wintertime underground, plumping themselves up with moisture. As winter retreats, the flowers of the bulb emerge. Sometimes they're a bit ahead of schedule and get caught by late freezes and snowstorms. Don't stress about your tulips, hyacinths, crocuses, daffodils, or snowdrops. They've evolved to bloom at that tricky time when winter and spring wrestle for dominance. They can withstand frost and snow (even if some flower stems snap). If they couldn't, they'd be extinct. If a heavy, wet snow threatens your tulips at the height of perfection, by all means cover them with bushel baskets, buckets, card tables, or whatever sheltering device you have handy. But these early bulbs don't need a blanket to keep them warm; they grow and flower best during the cool, sunny days of spring.

LEFT: fall-blooming crocus belie the season with their springlike charms, contrasted by reddening plumbago foliage. RIGHT: Late spring-blooming Dutch iris pair attractively with variegated dogwood.

When things heat up, the spring bulbs finish their annual cycle by setting seed, soaking up the sun to provide energy for the next spring, and going through their ugly phase of unkempt, yellowing leaves. The best thing you can do is snap off their seedpods so they don't waste the energy, fertilize the plants to ensure a great display next spring, and ignore the yellowing leaves until they've turned brown. If you cut or pull off the foliage prematurely, you'll likely affect the bulb's ability to turn in a star performance next season. Live with it. By planting the bulbs farther back in beds—rather than right at the edge—emerging perennials will help camouflage the dying bulb leaves.

Summer doesn't spell the end of bulbs. Some even bloom in fall. The term bulb, by the way, refers to the enlarged roots that have evolved over time for each kind of bulbous plant. Some are categorized as true bulbs (tulips and lilies), some as corms (crocuses and gladiolus), some as rhizomes (irises), and others as tubers (dahlias). They all vary in shape and size, but they are all efficient storage containers. And the great thing is that they can sit dormant for months while they zip around the world, arriving at planting time at your neighborhood nursery. Then these hard brown chunks get buried, send out roots, plump up, and emerge above ground to grow and flower. I've always found that wondrous and wonderful.

The summer bulbs may be either hardy or tender, depending, once again, on where you garden. For most people, lilies, irises, and liatris can be treated as perennials. The rest of them— dahlias, cannas, elephant ears, caladiums, and gladiolus—must be dug after frost and their bulbs, corms, rhizomes, and tubers stored over winter.

Startling Flanders poppies seed themselves among an easy-care collection of classic bearded iris that are cut back and divided every four or five years.

I must warn you here about falling into a very bad habit concerning bearded iris. I adore these plants, so I feel protective toward them. Anyway, irises grow quickly, and to keep them healthy and blooming, you need to divide them every four or five years. After they flower in late spring, you dig up a clump and break up the rhizomes into pieces about six inches long with a single "fan" of leaves. You replant each fan right near the soil surface with 6" to 8" between each piece. Now here's the important part: Because the rhizome has a lot of work to do in getting its roots reestablished, you help out by cutting the fan of leaves down by half with scissors. The roots can't support all that top growth. If you follow these directions, you'll grow superb iris. However, never cut back the foliage unless you're transplanting the iris. For some odd reason, millions of Americans think they should go out after these bloom and punish their iris for a job well done by disfiguring the leaves and cutting off half of their system of making food. If I see you've done it, I'll knock on your door and give you a stern lecture. I travel extensively, so don't think you're safe just because you live in Salt Lake City or Sheboygan.

Summer- and autumn-flowering bulbs make amazing contributions to the garden and patio pots. I'm especially fond of cannas, lilies, and dahlias in big pots as exotic, colorful exclamation points on terraces and patios. Often overlooked, fall-blooming bulbs add enchantment to our gardens late in the season. Put a note in your daytimer to buy and plant them in late summer and early fall. It's worth the effort. Fall crocuses bring a touch of spring to our beds and borders even as the backdrop changes to yellow and bronze. Springing from the earth without leaves, these pretty flowers are ideally planted in concert with low-growing ground cover perennials such as thyme, partridge feather, and plumbago. Unusual in their life cycles, these bulbs send up their leaves in spring, soak up the sun, and disappear until their surprise late performance.

HERBS: USEFUL AND BEAUTIFUL

It used to be that the only herbs most folks encountered were lavender in their soaps, some mint in their juleps, and perhaps some parsley garnishing their dinner plates. Thank goodness those days are gone. As we all hunger for a healthier, tastier diet, herbs have become invaluable in our kitchens. We find them in many facets of our lives, from the medicine cabinet to the bathtub and the linen closet. Many people classify herbs as the "useful plants," whether they're used for culinary, cosmetic, medicinal, or household purposes.

An herb garden can be a charming garden room. Alternately, herbs lend themselves to growing in borders or vegetable and cutting gardens as well as pots. One big misconception that you may have heard

> As we all hunger for a healthier, tastier diet, herbs have become invaluable in our kitchens.

An unusual "scare camel" protects a country garden that rivals those in southern France for charm, with its casual mix of lavender, daisies, poppies and ornamental onions.

repeated is that herbs like terrible soil and tough conditions. This, of course, depends on your soil type, but I guess it stems from the fact that many popular cooking herbs come from the Mediterranean region. Oregano, thyme, tarragon, rosemary, lavender, savory, and sage love full sun, don't need much water, and prosper in a mineral-rich, not-too-fluffed-up soil. To some people, that means poor soil; but for most of us, that's what we've got. Other herbs such as basil or ginger like organically rich, moist soil. Herbs display the same diversity as any other group of plants but, in general, are quite adaptable. Many that you wish to grow may thrive happily in a room devoted strictly to them. As you grow and experiment with this fascinating group, your kitchen and home will change forever.

TURF: WISE CARE

One of my summer chores growing up was tending the lawn. I hated it. But I learned what it took to have a healthy lawn with minimal effort (never underestimate an adolescent who'd rather be doing something else). Fertilize and aerate in spring and fall. Dig dandelions by hand the minute they start to bloom. Water during the coolest part of the day. And water infrequently and deeply to encourage the roots to delve deeply in search of water. Roots near the surface burn up. Set the mower blade at the highest level, the better to shade the roots during hot weather.

I've stood by these early findings ever since, and I've always had healthy, resilient lawns with a minimum of crabgrass (which I also hand-dig before it goes to seed) and never an instance of mold, fungus, or the other horrors that seem to plague overwatered grass. An inch of moisture a week is not only sufficient but also advisable for a tough turf that can roll with the punches. If you get moss in parts of your lawn, consider this: perhaps nature is telling you that moss would be more suitable than turf. Some of the most beautiful "lawns" I've seen in New England were made of moss.

I've recently reached a point in my life where I am lawn-free. The recent western drought pushed me over the edge. I don't begrudge anyone else's right to enjoy their lawn for family activities and, perhaps, the pleasure of tending it. Just do it responsibly and wisely to get the most out of your work and water. Many seasoned gardeners I know have little or no lawn. It all starts by expanding the borders by a foot or two. Sometimes a gardening couple will argue about whether this is necessary (husbands tend to treasure the time spent with their lawns), but eventually the border prevails.

As you plan your new garden, you may be starting with nothing more than a lawn. Ask yourself, "Do I really want that responsibility, to maintain a lawn up to the neighborhood standard?" It's work. Flower and vegetable gardening is work, too, but a lot less monotonous, and (in my opinion) infinitely more rewarding. Limiting the size of turf areas reduces water consumption and allows you to better care for what you've got. Eventually, I'd guess, you'll be nibbling away at the edges to make more room for flowers.

GROUND COVERS AND TURF ALTERNATIVES: ALONE OR TOGETHER

While various kinds of turf are the ultimate ground covers, a number of low-growing, low-maintenance perennials can serve much the same purpose. They're not suitable for badminton or dodgeball, but they offer a pretty alternative to the big stretch of green lawn. They're also

A tapestry of ground covers on a rocky slope includes sedums, snow-on-the-mountain, and ice plants, punctuated by flaming Oriental poppies.

ideal for slopes, hills, and irregular terrain that may be a challenge to mow. You can choose to plant a single ground cover, such as a moss or thyme. Or you can plant many kinds of ground covers as a tapestry of intertwining colors and textures. The best ground covers for your area will be found at your local nursery. Widely grown kinds include creeping veronica, thyme, brass button, ivy, lily turf (*Liriope*), pachysandra, lamium, vinca, wine cup, partridge feather, creeping baby's breath, mat daisy, Irish and Scottish moss, creeping phlox, hen and chicks, sedum, and ice plant. In addition, many require less water than most lawn grasses and little or no fertilization. And you never need to mow. Your world will become a quieter place.

■ Your Style

Never give up your vision. Style transcends climate. Almost everything is possible, budget and patience permitting. At the same time, consider the region in which you live and its natural landscape, as well as its signature plants—whether native (meaning indigenous) or not—that provide its gardening identity. After all, what's Portland without roses, Phoenix without saguaro cacti, New Orleans without bougainvillea vines, Richmond without dogwood trees, Denver without

Style transcends climate. Almost everything is possible, budget and patience permitting.

Southwestern gardeners draw on the desert and Native American cultures for inspiration, as strong architectural plants make a bold style statement.

blue spruce, or Washington, D.C., without cherry trees? The gardening heritage of your city or state may be an important factor in determining the style and contents of your garden.

The architecture of your home also figures into that determination. My modest turn-of-the-century cottage would look downright silly with a Louis XIV clipped ornamental garden, complete with formal pools and statuary. Conversely, a naturalistic meadow would appear equally out of place surrounding a stately brick Tudor home. We all borrow from other places and other times when conceiving our garden visions. Translating them into reality is what it's all about. For example, my garden is a hybrid between the classic perennial border garden and a cottage garden. Some might claim, "You can't do an English garden in Denver!" (or Kansas City or Charlotte or wherever you live). But they've disregarded the fact that any style of garden is simply that—a style. Had I planted mine with plants that thrive in England, I'd be doomed to failure. As it is, my English-themed garden has a Colorado twist, featuring flowers that survive and thrive in my dry, hot-in-summer, cold-in-winter climate. Plants don't know or care about style; they're satisfied when they get the right spot in the right garden.

■ Garden Rooms

Rooms organize a house. Most of us bathe in one room, cook in another, sleep, do laundry, play, read, and watch TV in others. Some rooms do double duty. Others don't do much. Unlike its namesake, for instance, the living room is often the least lived-in room in the house.

Rooms can also organize a garden (and they are really "living" rooms), even if they're not strictly for daily activities. When I'm in the garden, I'd just as soon ignore dirty dishes, piles of laundry, and the day's top stories. Time spent in a garden is unlike any other activity. Some days it's all about color and excitement. Others are about manicuring and attention to details. War is occasionally declared on weeds, while every once in awhile a day is dreamy and peaceful.

My garden is organized into several rooms. Some are for the pleasure and convenience of people, others for the specific requirements of the plants in them (shade, sun, moisture, etc.). As with the rooms of a house, these garden rooms demand care and attention. Like an interior designer who creates a room, I rarely get to use it the way it's intended. I'm more of a maid with dirty nails and knees. But that's my own fault: I've made my (garden) bed, now I must lie in it.

When friends come over, I'm forced to enjoy my garden. While I join in the conversation, music, and wine, however, I'm secretly thinking that the flowering maple over there is looking droopy and I've just got to get those bug-bitten leaves off the golden sweet potato vine. And that begonia really ought to be deadheaded. Right now! Pretty gardens do require time and the right kind of work at the right time. But perhaps the emphasis I've placed on the work involved to create one is misleading. It's not really work, after all, if it's something you enjoy. A garden is much more than a place in which to work. It's a place to live.

PLANNING A GARDEN ROOM

Let's focus on creating a garden room for a well-balanced, moderately industrious gardener. What do you plan to do in your garden room? In a conventional house, the activities are already assigned by room before we even move in. Their size, shape, fixtures, and location already determine how they're to be used. A stove or a tub is a good indicator. The rooms without appliances give us a little more wiggle room to turn them into something besides a spare bedroom, such as a library, sewing room, or home theater.

A garden room starts from scratch. At the start, the only thing that it has in common with an indoor room is a floor. In most cases, it has no walls, windows, ceilings, furniture, or ornaments. Sometimes, such as in the city, walls of other buildings define the garden space. New

A former concrete patio slab has been transformed into a peaceful room—perfect for knitting— with the addition of brick pavers, comfy wicker, and pots of blue lily-of-the-Nile.

Yorkers know all about this. But many people simply have a "yard," which is usually the lawn, trees, and shrubs that surround the house. The closest most yards get to having a room is the patio, oftentimes a concrete afterthought tacked onto the back of the house.

A real garden room can serve as an extension of the home. Your lifestyle will help you decide how it should be designed, whether for dining, entertaining, catnapping, or all of the above. Creating one room leads to another. Any garden appears larger when it's segmented and all is not apparent at first glance. Other garden rooms can be simply for display, showcasing a collection of plants the way we display trophies, books, and figurines inside. Taking the concept of a room too literally, collectors sometimes find a way to clutter it up with non-plant items. Take the case of an elderly couple I once saw on British TV who collected more than 500 gnomes. The broadcast showed them demolishing their collection with sledgehammers. When asked why, the lady of the house replied, "It got to be a bit much, really." I'm sure there's a lesson for all of us in this.

Getting back to the business of creating a room, the only thing that is absolutely necessary is a sense of enclosure. This can start perhaps with a wall or walls of a building and include fences, pillars, planters, and screens as well as living elements such as hedges and potted plants. Most of us don't like to sit in a room without windows (except at the movies) so the enclosure doesn't need to be thorough. A garden room doesn't necessarily need a ceiling, but it becomes more intimate with some sort of canopy, whether it's a tree, arbor, pergola, or even an umbrella.

> **I'd rather dine in a garden than in the fanciest restaurant in the world.**

DINING IN THE GARDEN

When I picture creating a garden room, I think about food. I'd rather dine in a garden than in the fanciest restaurant in the world. For one thing, I'm already dressed for it. For another, a summer's evening breeze scented by lilies or angel's trumpets enhances any meal (even one I cook). But even great tastes and scents are secondary if you're uncomfortable, so consider what you and your guests will sit on for a meal in an outdoor dining room. Teak, wrought iron, and cast aluminum—they're all great choices, depending on your taste. I don't go in for plastic—it just doesn't fit in with any of my garden concepts—but because this type of furniture is inexpensive, you can use it initially until you can find and afford what you really like. Furniture makes a design statement in a garden dining room. Sometimes it says, "French café," "English tea time," "Southern elegance," or "Laguna Beach lunch." I'm not exactly sure what mine says except maybe, "This looks comfy," mainly due to cushions and pillows. I'm constantly shuttling them inside when rain clouds appear, but they help to set a mood.

Mood is what a garden room is all about. You create it. It's a room like no other, always changing. And what's even better, a little dirt is perfectly acceptable. Some of my favorite moments have been spent in my outdoor dining room, never mind my compulsive gardening and inability to relax. I recall chili on a cold day, a cool salad on a warm night, the excitement of planting containers each spring, and just hanging out with my pets. I love watching the cats stalk butterflies and the dogs snoozing under the table or "helping" me with watering and deadheading.

A garden room isn't just about entertaining and relaxing. I don't relax much in the vegetable and herb room. I sweat. There's a chair and table in the shade to take a break, but the focus here is production. Though some people integrate vegetables and herbs into the rest of the garden, many gardeners like a separate area dedicated to them. Or they put vegetables and flowers for cutting together (a cutting garden). Some of us just find it too difficult to pick from the garden for fear it would spoil the show. I'm reluctant to pick from my main borders, too.

■ Beds and Borders

Let's talk about beds and borders. What's the difference? There really isn't much. A bed is usually a flat patch of ground, often carved out of the lawn. Traditionally, it displays bright

Where no rules apply, annuals, perennials, and shrubs stuff beds (or are they borders?) carved informally from the lawn. The plantings include roses, lupines, black-eyed Susans, penstemons, and dianthus.

summer annuals, such as petunias and geraniums, commonly known as "bedding" plants. At one time, when Britannia ruled the waves and Queen Victoria sat on the throne of England, bedding was all the rage. You could show off your wealth based on how grand, intricate, and labor-intensive your garden beds were. We don't see much of this in home gardens any longer, but remnants of it linger in municipal parks every summer. Occasionally a town or city will spell out its name in marigolds, for example. A local hotel tried this a couple of years ago using petunias. It was fairly legible as you drove by in early summer, but as the petunias grew and spread, the hotel name became a blur. The Victorians had enormous gardening staffs to snip and clip. At any rate, we don't bed so much these days.

By contrast, we make borders. A border is largely a European concept, especially English, which replaces beds of annuals with beds of perennials. We'll talk about these kinds of plants in detail later in the book, but suffice it to say that perennials live for many years and come up "perennially" each year, while annuals usually live up to their name and must be planted anew each year. By the very word "border," you might imagine that this piece of ground borders something, such as a wall, walkway, or property line. It can, of course, border something, but it's come to mean an arrangement of perennials usually in long, rectangular expanses. My "borders" are really just two equal strips of earth about 60' by 10' with a path down the middle. Some people like lawns running down their borders or a layer of fine pea gravel that crunches as you walk. A border can run alongside a driveway or fence, go uphill if it has to, and it doesn't even have to be straight. Borders traditionally have some sort of backing to them such as a wall or hedge. A lot of the English ones employ romantically crumbling brick walls. Mine has a picket fence. Whatever it is, the backing serves as a sort of device like a picture frame to set off the beauty of the plants.

> **Most of us are essentially cottage gardeners when we start, and after years of experimentation—becoming increasingly sophisticated—we often return to our cottage roots.**

Though a border used to be strictly about perennials, it's come to include just about every kind of plant you'd like to toss in it. This "mixed border" concept is a boon to kitchen-sink gardeners like me who wish to incorporate roses, tulips, basil, and anything else we fancy.

The most important part about a border is its complete lack of regimentation. This means no rows and essentially no strict rules. A beautiful border does, however, need a bit of discipline both in its planning and maintenance to keep from looking chaotic. For that we'll discuss colors, shapes, textures, and the sequence of blooms—later.

You've probably heard about "cottage gardens" as much as borders. They're planted just about the same as borders, really, but I'd say that they're especially exuberant and expressive. A famous British garden writer once called cottage gardens "undisciplined masses of flopping vegetation." When they became all the rage, he wrote a glowing book about them. Most of us are essentially cottage gardeners when we start, and after years of experimentation—becoming increasingly sophisticated—we often return to our cottage roots. I used to care far more about clever combinations. Last summer, I accidentally grew a blood red dahlia in a pot with magenta petunias, chartreuse sweet potato vine, and orange cigar plant. It was absolutely hideous and I didn't give a hoot. I'm definitely back to my exuberant cottage phase.

■ Rocks in the Garden

Rock gardeners are just cottage gardeners with rocks. They specialize in smaller plants, often from mountainous areas, that grow best amongst rocks, especially in the crevices. Rock gardeners almost always display meticulous grooming techniques as well as a huge thirst to try new plants. Gardening with rocks is a bit different than pure rock gardening. Many people garden with natural rock formations on their properties. Others haul in rocks to pay homage to the natural landscape of their regions.

My sister and I did this—in our own ways—when we were kids. On family trips to the mountains, we were allowed to bring home rocks we collected. Betty and I managed some fairly large-sized rocks that we put in the back of our family station wagon. We saved those for our rock gardens, which we planted with creeping phlox and hen and chicks and populated with

Stone, wood, and water characterize a Japanese-inspired garden, with breathtaking water lilies inviting reflection.

our pet turtles. My sister and I built rock gardens all over the place. It's great to have gardening parents who don't worry about what the neighbors think of their children's latest creation.

Japanese and Chinese styles of gardens often employ rocks in their designs, but for entirely different reasons than creating plant habitats. Many gardeners enjoy bringing Asian elements into their home gardens, as well as evoking the styles of planting. Stone, wood, and water can be used in many ways to evoke an Asian look. One word of caution: the architecture of your home must lend itself to these styles. Simplicity of line and ornament is critical to do justice to your interpretation of a Japanese garden surrounding your home. My understanding is that Japanese gardens, in particular, serve as artistic microcosms of the natural world. Before you do a sand garden or throw up a teahouse, investigate this discipline of gardening thoroughly. As with European styles of gardening, use plants suitable to your region in an Asian-inspired garden.

■ Naturalistic Gardens

Wherever you live, you'll find gardens that mirror the natural landscape. One of the strongest garden movements today is about prairies, plains, and meadows. There aren't many left of the virgin grasslands that used to cover so much of this continent. Cornfields and pastures have largely supplanted the plains. I have a particular appreciation for the plants I grew up with on the plains. From the edge of town where we lived, an endless sea of grasses stretched to the horizon.

Prairie and meadow gardens strive to present the beauty of these habitats. Besides the predominant grasses, these gardens also feature many of the wildflowers that, because of their toughness and beauty, have become garden stalwarts throughout the world, such as Indian blanket, goldenrod, aster, gayfeather, and coreopsis.

Most flowers were once wild, except for those "bred in captivity." Through breeding and selection, plants from around the world have blossomed into the ones that we grow in our gardens today. Hybrid tea roses, for example, aren't to be found just growing down by the side of the ditch. As "wild" subjects, many forerunners of modern hybrids look quite different. Modern dahlias, zinnias, and marigolds (all native to Mexico) have become big, bold, and brassy in comparison to the original wild plants. For many gardeners, the charm of the originals far outweighs the "improvements" by breeders.

These are what we usually think of when we picture wildflowers. They vary from region to region, of course, with some having a very large range and others being quite localized. Many

A rustic fence is all that separates these "captive" columbines from the untamed woods beyond; seedlings will likely jump the fence in the coming years.

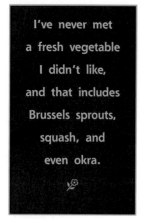

I've never met a fresh vegetable I didn't like, and that includes Brussels sprouts, squash, and even okra.

gardeners enjoy going "native," planting and growing the wild species of their regions. Already adapted to your soil and climate, they will probably prove to be tough and enduring.

■ Garden Edibles

Despite the fact that this introduction to gardening does not focus on edible plants, I wanted to be sure to offer a few tips to those of you who will not be content with a strictly ornamental garden. Growing up in a gardening family gave me an appreciation for working in the soil, even at a very early age, and for more than just growing plants. I also liked hoeing rows, planting seeds, and especially harvesting. Kids are notoriously fussy about eating vegetables (and often turn into fussy adults). But children in gardening families never need to be prodded to eat their peas, beets, or beans.

I've never met a fresh vegetable I didn't like, and that includes Brussels sprouts, squash, and even okra. I salivate just writing about homegrown corn and tomatoes. The popularity of farmer's markets testifies to our appreciation of freshly picked vegetables. As soon as a vegetable is picked, its sugar begins to turn to starch and the flavor fades. Carrots, corn, and peas are decidedly more delicious if eaten straight from the garden (or, in my case, in the garden; peas rarely make it to the kitchen).

Taste isn't the only reason to raise your own vegetables. With the tremendous popularity of pesticide-free, organically grown produce, it makes sense to raise your own healthy crops. The key is not to panic at the arrival of the first aphid. You can manage outbreaks of pests using soap. That's right, soap. Pure garden soap that you mix with water is available at garden centers. It doesn't poison insects, but instead dissolves their hard exoskeletons. Like the Wicked Witch of the West, they melt away. Explain that to your kids and they'll be thrilled to help spray the soap.

While pests are always a cause of concern, the most important aspect of growing vegetables is your soil. Although a loose, friable (crumbly) soil is ideal, a lack of it doesn't mean you're out of luck. Homeowners with heavy clay soil and high-rise dwellers without any soil at all have options. Raised beds filled with fertile topsoil can be created, and heavy soils can be improved by incorporating organic matter. And almost anybody with a balcony that receives at least a half-day's sun can grow vegetables in containers.

Root crops such as beets, turnips, carrots, onions, and radishes grow best in very loose soil with the consistency of store-bought potting soil. They have a difficult time extending their roots into heavy or rocky soil. Raised beds and large containers provide that ideal, loose growing medium.

As you plan your vegetable garden, choose a spot that receives plenty of sun. Some people don't consider a vegetable garden very pretty and hide it behind the garage or along the alley. Don't fall into that trap. Find the best spot for growing vegetables and turn it into a beautiful space. It can hold its own as a viable garden room if you enclose it with nice fencing or hedges, dress it up with ornaments such as a birdbath (birds should always be welcome to dine on insects), and create an interesting layout with paths and paving. Trellises and arbors add further architectural interest and support climbers such as pole beans, peas, and squash. Many gardeners add flowers to their vegetable garden, especially edible ones such as pansies, nasturtiums, and sweet Williams.

Vegetables are split into two groups: cool-season and warm-season. At the beginning of the growing season (cool season), depending on where you live, you can plant seeds or transplant young nursery seedlings of lettuce, spinach, peas, beets, radishes, and onions. They can withstand a light frost—even snow—and develop rapidly during cool, sunny weather. When the real heat hits (warm season), spinach and lettuce will bolt (send up flowering stalks), and their usefulness is over. Radishes become bitter and woody and peas cease flowering and become magnets for spider mites. Pull up these cool-season plants and compost them, and plant heat-loving vegetables in their place. Warm soil is essential for beans, corn, and squash to germinate well.

More tomatoes succumb to bad judgment about timing than any other crop. Peppers are right up there, too. Don't jump the gun: One unseasonably hot day doesn't mean it's safe to plant your warm-season crops. Tomatoes and peppers grow so quickly that even those planted in early June in northern gardens and in mountainous areas will rapidly catch up and soon surpass plants set out too early. Neither can stand one degree below freezing, and cool nights will stunt their growth for the entire season. Pay attention to the night temperatures in your area—they must stay reliably above 50 degrees; daily highs are irrelevant.

My best tip for growing great tomatoes (the favorite of most gardeners) is to bury a young transplant all the way up to its set of lower leaves. Tomatoes root all along the stem this way, ensuring a sturdy, well-rooted plant. Keep the soil evenly moist, feed regularly with a fertilizer formulated especially for tomatoes, and pick and stomp pesky tomato hornworms. Nothing beats the taste of a homegrown tomato. Each bite is memorable. I can almost taste it now.

■ Container Gardening

For everything you want to grow but don't think you can, there's container gardening. You control the soil, fertilizer, and water to accommodate most any plant you've been hankering to grow. The 300 pots on my patio and balcony are a testament to a lot of hankering.

Start with large pots of at least 10" or 12" diameters. Any smaller and you'll never be able to keep the soil within them moist (my small pots get good use housing my collection of succulents and cactus, which don't need much water). Terra-cotta pots "breathe," meaning that their porous walls allow both air and moisture to penetrate the walls. While that's beneficial to roots, it's not so good if the pots dry out on a hot day when you're not home. Containers made of fiberglass, wood, plastic, and glazed pottery don't breathe and consequently hold moisture better. Use potting soil (bags of commercially available soil labeled "potting soil" can be found at any nursery or garden supply store); garden soil rarely makes a suitable growing medium in pots.

You can create beautiful combinations of plants by blending upright, rounded, and trailing plants for a balanced effect. Plant them very tightly together for a lush look right off the bat. Fertilize every week to ten days to get great "magazine cover" results. Some plants may be best grown as single specimens in their own pots. They can then be grouped with other pots. I use bricks, blocks, and overturned pots beneath my

With container gardening you control the soil, fertilizer, and water to accommodate most any plant you've been hankering to grow.

A low stone wall elevates pots of flowers for an up-close experience, including oxalis, pink spider lily, pale pink Asiatic lilies, magenta stock, and white alstroemeria.

containers to stage them for the best show. I try to get many of them up to eye level so I can enjoy them when I'm dining or writing. Conversely, lower your hanging baskets so you're not just staring at the bottom of the basket.

Individual pots or groupings of them serve as focal points in the garden, disguise eyesores, direct traffic flow, provide screening, and mainly beautify our outdoor living spaces. Though we think of container plantings essentially for summer color, they're useful anytime, not only in frost-free climates but in cold ones as well. Holly, evergreens, and ornamental grasses can be especially attractive with a light dusting of snow. Also, containers can host dwarf fruit trees, evergreens, flowering shrubs, bulbs, and almost everything else that is ordinarily grown in the ground. (Rooftop and balcony gardeners need big pots and planters for some of these options.)

■ Watery Effects

A pond, reflecting pool, or fountain serves as cooling relief from summer's heat and glare. Gardeners' ponds play a vital role for birds, both for drinking and bathing. Even if you have no intention of ever installing a water feature in your garden, at least provide a bowl of clean water. The birds will revel in it and repay you by eating your unwanted insects.

When you do take the plunge and become a water gardener, you'll enter an exciting new world with its own lingo. Soon, you'll talk liners, pumps, filters, fish, and algae like a pro. You'll fall in love with water lilies and my favorite, the lotus. With its graceful blue-green leaves and elegant pink flowers, it's no wonder the lotus was used by ancient Egyptians as a recurring artistic motif.

Beyond water lilies and lotus, a pond may host many beautiful aquatics, especially those plants that thrive at water's edge. Some are hardy and may be planted directly in the mucky soil where their roots stay perpetually wet, while others are kept in their pots and submerged below water level. Among the loveliest of these plants are Japanese and Louisiana irises as well as *Iris pseuda-corus*, the fabled yellow fleur-de-lis of France. Rushes, reeds, and cattails are also perfect for the water's edge, along with tropical elephant ears (*Colocasia*), pickerel, papyrus, and water cannas. The dramatic foliage of rodgersias and ligularias can be stunning, topped by pink or golden flowers, respectively. Some water plants simply float. Water hyacinth, water lettuce, and duckweed migrate around the pond with the breeze. The first two should only be allowed in enclosed ponds, as they have become major pests in the South, escaping into and clogging waterways.

Deciding what sort of water feature you want is the most important part. It takes a deft touch to pull off a naturalistic pond. Unless you have a lot of space (in full sun, by the way), it's difficult to make your pond convincing. How many of us city dwellers have a natural spring and a rock outcropping in our backyards? In the country or where there are hills and rock formations, the illusion is far more convincing, but a more formal approach may work best for most of us.

A convincingly naturalistic pond teems with life such as an orange canna, rushes, water lilies, and golden yellow ligularia.

My raised pond, about 4' by 8', doesn't pretend to be natural. It has provided me with hours of entertainment as well as some strange encounters. You may meet some big birds. Herons may come for a tasty meal. A light on your pond at night is the equivalent of the famed golden arches to night-flying herons. Some water gardeners resort to netting over their ponds, but the best idea comes from my friends Susan and Rhonda, who bought black plastic boxes (about the size of a bread box) at a home improvement store. The boxes, intended for some sort of plumbing, have holes for tubes and pipes so the fish can swim in and out and hide inside. It works like a charm.

Raccoons regularly mug my pond. Whether it's to wash or eat (there always seem to be fewer fish after one of their visits), they just trash my pond. I put mousetraps on the pond's edge to deter them. The fish population seems to rebound from the predations and only once have I needed to start from scratch. Several winters ago, a warm day lured my goldfish to the surface. The temperature plunged suddenly, trapping them in the ice. This is known as the "great fish stick episode." The adventure continues.

■ Color Basics

We've talked plenty about plants, although barely mentioning what draws us to them: color. We're all so different. And we see color differently. Some of us are cautious or confused about color. Others, like me, tend to collect one or two kinds of plants and give scant thought to color combinations. Then there are the magpies, who are attracted to bright, shiny objects, and have one of everything. There are also the minimalists, whose color palette is extremely limited. And finally, there are those with a "survival garden," where the color scheme is based on what hasn't died.

Unfortunately, too many of us never find out what we really like because we're scared to experiment. Whether it's our home, wardrobe, or garden, we're so unsure and afraid of making mistakes that we limit ourselves before we even start. Many people stick with the equivalent of a black cocktail dress. They play it safe.

Comparing colors of apparel and garden flowers isn't quite fair, but I think people confuse them. You have no idea how many times I've heard a client say, "I hate orange," or "I loathe yellow." It's too bad that somewhere between our first box of crayons and adulthood we learned to hate a particular color. I have to respect this prejudice, of course, but on what is it based? If it's because you look hideous in yellow or orange, don't wear it. Clothing is next to our skin and hair; flowers bloom against a green background.

> To begin experimenting with color, take one base color and repeat it over and over in your plantings.

Coats of color paint the garden throughout the season. Planning helps to match them with the appropriate time. Our psychological needs should be considered in the process. In northern states, for example, gardeners are hungry—no, ravenous—for spring color after a monochromatic winter. In summer, blues and lavenders provide a slight respite from the heat. And in fall, gold and orange match our moods, even if they might seem out of sync at any other time. There's no reason to exclude any color from the garden; just find the season where it best fits.

The palette of spring plantings can be among the weirdest. Maybe it's because the fall-planted bulbs aren't ever compared with the perennials with which they'll bloom until they erupt into a big spring clash. After all, a tulip is just a picture on a bag when we plant it. Small wonder that some combinations are excessively cheerful. Red tulips and basket-of-gold are the visual equivalents of nails on a chalkboard to me. Yellow daffodils and hot pink creeping phlox I find equally disturbing. I actually like this perennial and employ it frequently, especially soft pink 'Candy Stripe' and 'Emerald Blue', although the latter is so deceivingly named. Its color is delicate lavender-blue. (The color peacemakers in the garden are blue, purple, or lavender.) I've usually found that almost all pastels go together without much trouble and that all intense colors—let's call them jewel tones—work well together.

Because color can be so personal and so emotional, I don't believe in assigning rules about it. Even if I did, I also believe that rules are for breaking. There are some tips, however,

Pretty in pink, these Asiatic lilies, pincushion flowers, and rose campion get a boost from the chartreuse leaves of variegated yucca and golden hops vine.

that can help a bit when approaching color. To begin experimenting with color, take one base color and repeat it over and over in your plantings. This is similar to painting the walls of a room with a consistent color. Since we were discussing lavender-blue anyway, consider how soothing it is and how many perennials and shrubs feature lavender-blue flowers, from veronicas and catmints to salvias and butterfly bushes. This color can span the seasons, providing a base for adding bolder jewel tones.

The same base color could be pink, yellow, or white. Then you can go off in any direction that suits you and the season. In the case of lavender-blue, add some deeper blues and purples and you've set the stage for hot pink or coral accents, or perhaps even orange. Oddly enough, if you take the base colors of pink, yellow, or white and add darker blues and purples, you've set up exactly the same situation. A base color plus purple is the ideal way to incorporate jewel tones into the garden, whether they're golden California poppies, ruby roses, magenta wine cups (*Callirhoe involucrata*), or orange tiger lilies.

The base color idea is also practical for those who collect plants that span a wide color range, such as irises or lilies. Sometimes these flowers come in unusual shades—or several at one time—that are a bit hard to fit in gracefully. A simple base color background pulls it all together. For the magpie gardeners, who are attracted to bright colors and pick up one of this and one of that until their gardens look like button collections, add a base color to make some semblance of order out of the hodgepodge. This could be as simple as broadcasting (i.e., spreading) a half pound of bachelor's buttons or sweet alyssum seeds (in a single color, not a mix) to fill in the gaps and provide unity.

Minimalist schemes are often great experiments—in the beginning. If you create a garden room that's limited in color (and you become as tired of it as I became of my all-white border), try adding the equivalent of throw pillows. Toss in one new color each season—even if it's just a foliage contrast—such as lime green in an all-yellow garden or burgundy in all-pink or -red one.

Finally—and you know who you are—there are those with a color scheme based on what's left from what you planted last year. Plenty of gardens start out with lovely color schemes, but the voles ate the tulips, the daisies croaked last winter, and the astilbe succumbed during the drought. What's left doesn't hang together. I've seen living rooms like this too. The walls used to match the sofa that the cat shredded, and the new chintz chairs were such a great deal, even though they're not that great with the plaid upholstery on the new sofa.

Let's make it simple. Pick one accent foliage color, such as silver, and three colors (make one of them bright) say pale pink, powder blue, and magenta. If you've already planted, dig out everything that doesn't fit this scheme and give these strays to your neighbors. Go to the nursery. Splurge.

■ Think Ahead When Buying

Keep in mind that summer and fall flowers are not in bloom in spring; two-thirds of your purchases should be for coming seasons. Spring may seem like an odd time to plan for fall color in the garden, but each autumn we do the reverse, planting crocuses, daffodils, and tulips to greet us in spring. It makes sense to take advantage of our early-season enthusiasm to ensure a colorful garden late in the year.

Summer heat often puts a damper on planting. If it's hot and/or dry, it's both tiring and risky to plant perennials. And let's face it: We buy what's in bloom. Most people purchase their plants in spring. Blooming annuals and perennials fly off the garden center shelves. The gallon pots of later-blooming perennials, devoid of bloom, get passed by. If you truly want a profusion of bloom throughout the season, a full half of your spring purchases should be strictly green. That's right, no flowers. To do this, you need to do some homework. What late bloomers are suitable for your garden?

People who need instant gratification will need to steel themselves. It's difficult to resist color. If you buy smart, your garden will be as beautiful in September as in June, if not more so. Don't forget the crescendo effect: by combining annuals with late-blooming perennials, the color will intensify throughout the summer and into fall. Many annuals reach their peaks in late August and September, coinciding with the explosion of fall-blooming perennials. Annual zinnias, dahlias, gomphrenas, verbenas, sweet potato vines, and black-eyed Susans hit their stride just as perennial asters, mums, hummingbird trumpets, plumbagos, coneflowers, Japanese anemones, and ornamental grasses come into their own.

Planting late bloomers in spring gives them almost an entire season to grow and perform. Even small-sized plants, with proper care, can put on a great show, although they'll be even more amazing in coming years. There's an old saying about perennials: "The first year they sleep, the second year they creep, the third year they leap." They may leap a little faster than the old adage—depending on the attention and fertilizer you lavish upon them—but have patience for a year or two.

■ Weed Strategies

Dreams do come true in fairy tales (and sometimes in gardens), but it's usually after plenty of toil and suffering. In fairy tales, the usual cause of all the turmoil is the wicked stepmother. In gardens, it's the weeds. During the excitement of planning and planting, weeds aren't on our minds. We're dreaming of tulips and roses and tomatoes. How dare weeds give us a wake-up call?!

Everyone wants a magic "cure" for weeds. For the kind of garden I like and design, there isn't one. I don't use or recommend black plastic, landscape fabric, weed barrier cloth, or smothering bark nuggets. They're just not natural. The only way to achieve a real garden is with real sweat. And that means weeding.

Weeds are a fact of life. Whenever we turn a spadeful of earth, we're exposing opportunistic seeds. Developing a strategy for coping with them is part of making a new garden or enlarging an existing one. In one category are the really bad, horrible weeds. Whoever said that a weed is just a flower growing in the wrong spot must have been on heavy medication or never ran into the likes of bindweed, kudzu, bittersweet, thistle, and various ivies. You probably know about the worst thugs in your neighborhood. They're basically despised for their aggression, tenacity, and deep roots. In the other category are the pesky weeds, slightly less aggravating because of their annual nature. These include portulaca, wild lettuce, shepherd's purse, mare's tail, lamb's quarters, hen bit, dandelion, pigweed, and knotweed. It's funny that so many carry picturesque—even cute— common names. Their greatest strength is in their numbers—kajillions of them.

I've never had the good fortune to start one of my own gardens on a piece of property that didn't host a couple of really bad thugs. Sometimes they've even fooled me into thinking I'd conquered them, only to discover they were just waiting until I'd planted before rearing their ugly heads again. My best piece of advice is to make sure they're good and dead before you plant. The method of killing them is up to you and depends on the nature of the villains.

The worst possible thing to do is to rototill if you're facing a persistent, deep-rooted weed such as bindweed. For a week or so, you'll pat yourself on the back. But soon every piece you chopped up will become a new weed. The best control for these sorts of weeds might be to use an herbicide or to smother them with a layer of plastic or newspapers for up to a year. My personal method is to pull them over and over—up to six times—to weaken the plant, then to hit them with an herbicide such as Round-up. My rampaging crop of bindweed appears to be (nearly) extinct, but the tree of heaven that came with

> Whoever said that a weed is just a flower growing in the wrong spot must have been on heavy medication or never ran into the likes of bindweed, kudzu, bittersweet, thistle, and various ivies.

the place sends out runners as effortlessly as most of us send e-mails. There's even one growing in my laundry room. Yes, in it. I've chopped, dug, and sprayed, but it's a battle of wills. Ordinarily I wouldn't credit a tree with the ability to form intent, but I do wonder when it mounts a home invasion.

When you've conquered the really tough weeds (or if you lucked out and never had to face them at all), the first-year garden still offers challenges. Weeding can take the fun out of the whole experience. It seems never-ending, as weeds of different kinds take their turns and germinate throughout the growing season. Many weed seeds can lie dormant for years or decades, just waiting for an opportunity.

My most persistent of the pesky weeds last season in a new garden area was portulaca. Springing up as thick as dog hair, this fleshy-leafed annual thrives in hot, dry weather, much like its ornamental cousin we usually call moss rose. There was nothing rosy about this picture. Whereas most annuals that I hoe or pluck have the decency to die, portulaca often re-roots. I like to use a tool called an "action" or "shuffle" hoe for annual weeds. It looks a bit like a horseshoe mounted on a handle, with a flat, two-sided blade that cuts just beneath the crust of the soil as you rake it back and forth. It's very useful, but I go back with a rake to pick up the portulaca before it roots again.

I went through about five rounds with the portulaca, cleaning out every last one before a new batch would sprout a week or so later. Cooler temperatures finally turned the tide in my favor, so I expect very little resistance this coming season. The perennials will begin to expand, shading much of the ground, leaving less and less opportunity for portulaca or any other weeds. The third year in a garden for me is generally almost weed-free, leaving more time for the more rewarding chores.

Weeding does have its good points, depending on how efficient you become. There are days I actually enjoy it. Good tools help. A really sturdy dandelion digger is perfect for tap-rooted weeds. Don't buy a cheap one; it won't last a week without bending. I rely heavily on my Japanese fisherman's knife, often called a hori-hori. It can serve for tap-rooted weeds as well as shallow-rooted weeds, because the edge is serrated to cut just below the soil surface. Several kinds of hoes are useful as well, from the previously mentioned hollow type to the standard flat blade or smaller dagger-pointed variety for tight spaces. And some people prefer their bare hands, wrestling victory from the earth in hand-to-hand combat.

Weeding takes up valuable time, so we need to make the most of it. I often play music on headphones. Sometimes I sing. My neighbors frown on this. During the attack of the portulaca, I used the reward system on myself. It goes something like this: "If I get as far as that butterfly bush (or whatever landmark selected), I'll stop for a while, sit in the shade, and possibly find the strength to go inside and find some chocolate." The weeds are gone and I'm still using this system. Now that's a happy ending.

■ Insects, Pests, and Diseases in the Garden

My parents never used insecticides in their garden, so I've grown up pretty ignorant of them. And I intend to keep it that way. People freak out at the sight of the first aphid of the year and overreact with an arsenal of chemical weapons. My advice? Chill. A bug-free garden is as unnatural as one made of artificial flowers. As I've mentioned before, soap is a gardener's best friend. I mix a teaspoon of Dr. Bronner's Castille Oil soap in a spray bottle with a quart of water and have at it. Spraying any pesky aphids I can see (you've got to hit them for the soap to dissolve them), I also make sure to hit the undersides of leaves and stems. This is where most sucking insects like aphids, spider mites, and white flies hang out.

Then there are the chewing insects like caterpillars, beetles, and earwigs. I hate earwigs. It's not that they do any more damage than any other bug; it's just that they're furtive like cockroaches with little pincers in front. I've seen enough science fiction movies to be totally creeped out by the threat they could pose to all humanity.

For every bad bug in the garden, there's one on your side. And along with the ladybugs, lacewings, predatory wasps, praying mantis, and spiders (the good guys) is the bird and bat brigade, which feasts on insects. Start to tinker with this coalition by introducing poisons, and you'll destroy the natural balance. Would you begrudge the caterpillars a meal or two before they transform into butterflies? And no matter how careful you are with chemical sprays and dusts, do you really want to take chances with children, pets, fish, and wildlife?

Of course, there may be critters that you would like to banish from your garden. Depending on where you live, perhaps you'll tangle with mice, squirrels, voles, moles, ground squirrels, gophers, rabbits, skunks, raccoons, deer, elk, or moose—or some combination thereof. Consult your local experts at botanical gardens, nurseries, and extension services on how best to deal with whatever is plaguing you. There are some truly destructive insects and critters out there with which I've never had to deal. Perhaps you may need to at some point. All I can say is that I'd urge you to take the most conservative approach. It never hurts to consult the seasoned gardeners in your neighborhood. Odds are, they've seen it all and may have some clever, environmentally friendly remedies. Approaches work differently in some regions and at certain times of the year.

Some of your staunchest allies are your pets. Both cats and dogs can be deterrents to wildlife, whether they're aggressive protectors or just hanging out on the porch. The mere scent of dogs, for example, puts off deer. I met a man in Montana with a beautiful garden out in the country that wasn't fenced (usually the only reliable way to keep deer out). He'd trained his dog since he was a puppy to mark certain trees and rocks that ringed the property. He and the puppy walked and peed several times a day for several months until it became part of the dog's daily routine.

Still, I'd recommend fencing for best results, since deer will eat the shingles off your house if they're hungry enough. Much is made of deer-resistant plants that they will find unpalatable, as well as soap sprays, hot pepper sprays, blood meal, sirens, flashing lights, and heavy metal music. I'd imagine you'd mostly alarm your neighbors rather than have a lasting effect on a herd of deer with appetites bigger than those of teenagers. I think deer are beautiful creatures when I see them in the mountains, but I can't imagine them grazing in my garden. I think they'd quickly lose their charm. So put up some substantial fencing or get a puppy and go for a stroll.

Plant diseases are no fun. Some are not usually life-threatening, such as mildew, although others such as clematis wilt are fatal. Can you prevent most diseases? Not really. Can you avoid the plants that get them? You bet. Nursing sick plants is grim and depressing. A garden full of mildewed, black-spotted plants is common, but unnecessary. In any region there are hundreds, no thousands, of plants that stay healthy no matter how humid and muggy it gets. Some books will recommend "good air circulation," as if you could place giant fans in pertinent spots in your garden. When plants succumb to disease, they're most likely ill-suited to growing in your region. You can become nursemaid rather than gardener or decide that no matter how lovely a plant might be (somewhere else) you can find a new love. And it's always worth investigating varieties that have natural resistance or have been bred to be resistant.

■ Realistic Maintenance

How much work your garden requires depends on its size, complexity, and the types of plants you grow. It also depends on your temperament. Some of us can easily overlook flaws. Others have this compulsive need to be on top of everything all the time, so we're constantly snipping and clipping. And timing is everything.

When I was five years old, my family moved to a small town on the eastern plains of Colorado. Gardening was a hard-fought battle on that windswept land. My early memories are of flowers, from the lilac and bridal veil bushes that hugged our house, to tulips and tomatoes in the garden, to wild roses and asters in the fields next to our house.

I've gardened for more decades than I care to admit, and it's still a sweaty and dirty business; but I no longer think in terms of war. Fighting nature is an exercise in futility. Accepting soil and weather conditions—and welcoming challenges—yields the most rewards. Knowing what to do—and when—makes gardening a pleasure rather than a chore (depending, of course, on how you feel about sweat and dirt).

Each spring I observe great mistakes. Apartment dwellers imagine their houseplants would appreciate a little sunshine as much as they do and drag them to the balcony; ficus trees and ferns bake to a crisp. Blooming delphiniums and roses fresh from the greenhouse get planted in suburban gardens way too early; a late snowstorm inevitably flattens them like pancakes.

The trickiest time of the gardening season begins in midspring. The key is to balance enthusiasm with caution. Starved for color after our winter abstinence, some of us plant recklessly without consulting the calendar. Each region has a set date considered to be that of the average last frost. In my region, May 15 is the green light to set out warm-season favorites such as tomatoes, peppers, marigolds, and zinnias. But May 15 doesn't come with a guarantee, and it's actually too late for the cool-season annuals such as peas, spinach, leaf lettuce, and pansies. This will likely prove true in your region as well.

In truth, the gardening season begins much earlier than most people think and ends much later as well. Learning what gets planted when—and where—is vitally important. Novice gardeners try to buy tulip bulbs in spring, never guessing that their window of opportunity closed in late fall. Sun-loving roses languish beneath a canopy of trees, while shade-loving hostas fry in a sunny hot spot. Yankees who move down south stick to their old habits and plant their pansies just in time to roast them to a crisp. There's no need. We all make mistakes, and good gardeners learn from them. Just avoid the obvious ones. If you're not killing some plants from time to time, you're not trying very hard to learn how to garden. Experience, of course, is the best teacher. I still kill my fair share of plants; it's just more embarrassing for me.

Perhaps we should talk a bit about shopping before we talk about the art of planting and the other garden skills. Shopping is one of my favorite parts of gardening. You say you're good at it? You'll make a great gardener. Shop in stores throughout the season and from winter catalogs

Imagine the pleasure of tending this productive plot devoted to squash and corn, as well as to flowers for cutting—cosmos, marigolds, and sunflowers.

and your garden will never be dull. I rarely see crummy, poorly grown plants at a nursery these days, so I'm not going to go into a long spiel about selecting healthy plants. Look for good foliage color and you might check beneath the leaves for bugs—but I don't do that, so why should you? There will probably be a few roots poking out from the drainage holes in the bottom of the plant's pot. That's fine. If they're longer than a few inches and the root ball is threatening to bust out, the plant is known as "pot bound." This hasn't ever stopped me from buying a plant. You simply take it home, cut it out of its plastic prison, and try to trim and help separate the roots a bit. Then give it a loving home in the ground or a new pot.

■ Basic Skills

There are a few basic skills to learn to become a good gardener. They're all easily mastered. Most become second nature in time. Intuition plays a big part in figuring out what to do and when. Avoid making work for yourself. If everything looks all right, let sleeping dogs lie. Don't go out and hack at your bushes just because you think you should be doing something.

> Whoever writes nursey tags for plants lives in a Camelot of gardening where plants reach amazing proportions never seen elsewhere.

PLANTING

Planting is the most important skill you can learn. Do it gently, but firmly. The best way to learn is to watch an experienced gardener at work. Go to a botanical garden if there's one nearby to observe. Better yet, volunteer so you can get hands-on experience.

To plant your newly purchased plants, dig a hole larger than the pots in which they came. Turn the pots upside down with one hand, holding the other hand underneath to catch them, and coax the plants out gently (gravity will do most of the work); no yanking and pulling out by the stems. Plant them at the same level that they're growing in their pots, but in a slight depression. Gently pack the soil around the plant, but no stomping. Just use the strength in your hands.

As you work, build a little mud wall about 2" high around each plant to capture moisture. "Puddle in" each plant with a very slow trickle of the hose until it's thoroughly saturated. Each plant is essentially still in its container, so water deeply each time, probably every four to seven days for a gallon-size perennial, depending on your soil and weather. If you live in a cold winter area, fertilize every couple of weeks through July, and then stop so the plants can begin to prepare for cooler fall weather. In their second year, perennials need little or no fertilizer.

TRANSPLANTING

There comes a time when you'll want to divide and transplant a perennial. This is best done in early spring just as the plant emerges, but hardly anybody gets around to it then. You can basically do it any time except during the real summer heat. Dig it up (a digging fork is easiest, but a shovel will do). Cut it in half or in several pieces depending on its size. The blade of a spade works well. Give it a hard thrust. You can also use a sturdy kitchen knife.

Transplanting is just like planting, except that you usually give your subject a haircut before you replant. This generally means cutting back the top growth so the roots don't have so much to support while they're reestablishing themselves. The plant should end up at the same level it was growing at before you started. Again, create an earthen dam around the base to catch and hold water and thoroughly soak the soil immediately after planting.

GROWING FROM SEED

Sowing seeds is much less work than planting. Some kinds can be simply sprinkled over the soil as if you were feeding chickens. I usually do this in either fall or late winter with annuals such as larkspurs, poppies, and bachelor's buttons. Vegetable seeds are usually but not always planted in rows, at the appropriate time for each kind. After digging and leveling the site with a rake, use a hoe to create a furrow 1" or so deep. Then plant the corn, peas, beans, or whatever you like, covering the seeds about a ¼" to ½" deep. Space the seeds a few inches apart, knowing that as they germinate and grow, you'll need to thin them to allow room for each one to develop. How much to thin depends on what you're growing. Radishes need only a few inches in between, while corn needs a foot.

Sowing seeds inside is a bit easier, mainly because you're sitting down. The easiest way for most of us is to fill plastic six-pack plant containers with a soil mixture especially formulated for seedlings. Plant a few seeds per cell (you'll need to thin later), covering them as directed on the seed packet. Water from the bottom by soaking the containers in their trays or you'll probably wash the seeds all over the place. Seed packets also tell you when to plant, generally four to eight weeks before the average frost-free date in your area, so count backward from that date. It helps to get this all organized on paper in midwinter, plus it gives us something to dream about when winter seems never-ending.

SPACING PLANTS

How much room your plants need between them is very tricky. I pay attention to the growth estimates for trees and shrubs and space accordingly. For perennials and annuals, I tend to follow my own instincts because I don't trust the nursery tags. Whoever writes them lives in a far-off Camelot land of gardening where plants reach amazing proportions never seen elsewhere. So for where I live in the mountain West, I cut the recommended spacing down by at least a third and sometimes by half. My theory is that most of us prefer results during our lifetimes.

Glorious dahlias result from pinching, staking, fertilizing, and deadheading. They're worth the fuss.

FEEDING PLANTS

Once everything is planted and growing, feed your plants. There's no set standard; some plants are heavier feeders than others. Some don't want or need any supplemental fertilization at all. Just as a general guideline, be generous with roses, bulbs, most annuals, containerized plants, and vegetables. Most trees, shrubs, vines, herbs, and perennials can get along pretty well on their own. Many people overfeed their perennials and end up with a bunch of lax, floppy plants. Then they have to stake them. I don't like staking and I rarely grow plants that are bred to fall over, but occasionally I make an exception. You probably will, too.

PLANT SUPPORTS

My weakness is dahlias. The tall ones need stakes. I grow them in pots on my patio for their huge, eye-popping blossoms in the heat of summer and into fall. I pinch my dahlias when they're about 6" tall. This means I tweak out the growing tip with my thumb and forefinger. This causes them to branch out and get bushy. Pinching is great to help avoid tall thin plants. Try it on petunias, flowering tobacco, pansies, flowering maples, and geraniums to get really floriferous plants. But back to stakes. When necessary—and before your lanky plant blows over—insert at the base a sturdy bamboo pole as tall as the plant is projected to reach. Use yarn, string, or twist-ties every 10", attaching it first to the stake and then around the plant stem. Sometimes I use tree branches with a "Y" joint (like one you'd use to make a sling-shot) and simply prop up a droopy plant. This kind of staking is barely noticeable. You can also buy metal supports and hoops. These are useful for top-heavy flowers such as peonies, which too often display their blossoms in the mud.

DEADHEADING, SHAPING, AND PRUNING

Most plants need grooming. The most common cleanup is deadheading, which has nothing to do with concerts. It's simply cutting or pinching off faded blossoms and their stems. The technique varies. For a Shasta daisy, for example, take off the flower and its long stem where it emerges from the base of leaves. For a begonia, just pinch off the spent flower. Deadheading encourages plants to keep blooming rather than putting their energies into seed production. Sometimes the entire plant is cut back to persuade it to regenerate and re-bloom. These summer cutbacks are for June bloomers that look tired and worn out in July. Now's your chance to do some serious whacking, cutting back many perennials by half or more—sometimes all the way to the ground. A list of candidates that prosper after a cutback (and a subsequent feeding) include many daisies, meadow sage, lupine, columbine, and catmint.

You can always do a bit of shaping and pruning when you like, but most people do too much. For most of us, early spring is the best time to cut out dead branches on trees and shrubs and do minimal shaping. This is also the time to cut back perennials and ornamental grasses. Meadows can simply be mowed. The old idea that the garden needs to be put to bed in fall has pretty much gone by the wayside. Save your autumnal energy for planting bulbs and moving pots of tropical plants inside. Nowadays we leave perennials, grasses, and even some annuals alone as winter comes, the better to enjoy their freeze-dried beauty. This also helps to protect the crowns of the plants from the extremes of winter.

■ Tips to Save Energy: Yours and the Garden's

The rhythm of a garden isn't a constant one. Nor is a gardener's. In spring most of us have energy to burn. That's good because there's plenty to be accomplished. Last year's perennials and grasses are cut back in mid- to late winter, depending on where you live. At about the same time, cool-season annuals and vegetables need to be sown outdoors. Peas, for example, are traditionally planted on St. Patrick's Day across the northern tier of states. In the meantime, many gardeners get a jump on the growing season by starting warm-season annuals and vegetables indoors.

The weather plays us like a yo-yo. It's too cold. Then it's warming up. No, wait—it's still too cold. Well, it feels pretty mild; maybe I should start transplanting and spading the vegetable patch. Oops, it's snowing. The moisture was good anyway. Now maybe it's okay. It was still pretty chilly last night. It's been 90 degrees for a week now. Oh dear, is it too late to plant tomatoes? This weather roller coaster can really wear you down. In the beginning of the season (spring, that is) we all invariably overdo it. We're not yet garden tough, so sore muscles and strained backs become common. Our bodies tone and strengthen as the season progresses. By mid-June, we're feeling pretty buff.

> In the beginning of the season (spring, that is) we all invariably overdo it. We're not yet garden tough.

Then it hits. The heat, humidity, grasshoppers, and crabgrass start to take their toll. We've reached the summer energy crisis. In what's supposed to be the time when we most enjoy our gardens, we can become too worn out. It seems only the super-gardener can shrug off the summer's setbacks to keep his or her garden picture-perfect. I'm no super-gardener, but my midsummer garden looks pretty cool. Here's how:

- Water plants in early morning, deeply and only when necessary (remember, poke your fingers into the soil to see how much moisture your plants have).
- Count on container plantings for color and substance (these are the plants you can most easily control); use tropicals and other heat lovers.
- Give your plants plenty of food and water (especially for the container plantings); install drip lines in the garden if you're mechanically inclined.
- Cut back early-blooming perennials.
- Select a different, small area to be groomed each day. Give it 20 minutes or whatever time you can. Move on to a new area the next day.
- Wear light-colored clothing along with broad-brimmed hats when you garden.
- Don't sweat the small stuff, such as deadheading. There's always next week.
- The best time to pull a weed is when you see it.

■ Essential Garden Tools

What tools do you need? Forgive me if I say, "It depends." There are some perfectly nice tools I've never used, so I can only tell you what I find "essential" and "nice to have." Let's start with the ones I use most. The Japanese fisherman's knife, called a hori-hori, features a 7" steel blade, serrated on one side, with a wood or plastic handle. Its primary uses include weeding, planting small stuff, and, presumably, gutting fish. A hori-hori costs about $20 to $35 depending on the model you get. Only one major caveat: Keep this tool out of reach of your children!

PRUNERS AND LOPPERS

The next essential is a pair of pruners, also called secauters by people who don't think pruners is descriptive enough. There are several different styles. I'd suggest a basic pair with a grip that feels comfortable. You'll get plenty of use out of a pair of pruners when you cut back the garden in spring, prune shrubs and small tree branches, deadhead flowers, and harvest herbs. I'd splurge and get a good pair (meaning, lifetime), for which you'll spend close to $50. Loppers are like bigger pruners and can handle slightly larger limbs up to about 1 ½" in diameter. They're nice to have around (I borrow my neighbors'). You can get a decent lopper for about $30.

DIGGING TOOLS

Still in the essentials, you need a spade or shovel (unless you're a rooftop gardener and never dig in the earth). The classic shovel is for digging. Buy a good quality one that won't break when you do something dumb like pry a boulder out with it. Of course, now you say you wouldn't do anything like that—but you will. You can buy a decent shovel at the hardware store for $15 and up. A rubber coating at the end of the handle may help prevent blisters. A spade has a flat spade. I like my "border" spade a lot. It cost about $50, and I'll probably have it forever. I mainly use it for dividing: once you've dug up a big clump of daylilies or whatever, a good thrust with the blade will cut it cleanly in half. For people of petite stature, try a lady's spade, which is a smaller version, or a border spade, which is pretty much the same thing. I like this tool for working in tight quarters to dig holes for bulbs or new perennials.

I also get good use from my digging fork. It looks a bit like a pitchfork, but has longer, thinner tines and is much lighter. A digging fork is a sturdy tool, usually with four or five steel tines that are designed to loosen a vegetable garden's soil before planting or to lift clumps of perennials for transplanting or dividing. A cheap version of this tool will bend when confronted by heavy, wet soil, hidden rocks or debris, or a really entrenched shrub rose that you've decided to move. So do invest in a better tool that will stand the test of time.

Since we're still discussing digging tools, I'd also spring for a good-quality trowel. Essentially a miniature, hand-held spade, a trowel is designed for digging small holes for things like perennials and annuals. A good strong handle and sturdy blade are necessary. You'll bend a cheap one in two days. The point of contention is where the handle meets the blade. If this isn't securely joined, it will fall apart. One-piece forged pieces of stainless steel get around this problem. Be prepared to pay at least $25 for a good trowel.

I occasionally use my dibble, which is a quaint tool for making uniform holes for seeds or small bulbs. It's essentially a pointed, plump piece of wood (like a swollen wooden carrot) that you can probably live without. But it does look picturesque on the potting bench. Speaking of which, do you need a proper potting bench? I admire the really nice ones immensely, with their stainless-steel tops and compartments for potting soil and stuff. I usually do my seeding on the dining table or kitchen floor and I plant my containers in place on the patio or balcony. Still, a potting bench would look really stylish in my sunroom.

RAKES

Most people rake more than I do; I lack the obsession to remove every leaf and blade of grass that falls. When I had a lawn, I used a mulching mower (which I highly recommend) to chop up the leaves in my last fall mowing. I leave most leaves where they fall in the garden itself to protect plants and disintegrate over the winter. This is a judgment call, because too many leaves can compact into a slimy mess that smothers rather than protects your plants. But

Even when its days of service are over, a leaky wheelbarrow positioned by the tool shed holds a bevy of beautiful daylilies, liatris, and 'Moonbeam' coreopsis.

to the subject of rakes: a lightweight, aluminum leaf rake is pretty much indispensable around your property (you can get back-saving ergonomic models, as you can with many kinds of tools as well as those for lefties). Even better for working among plants in fall or spring is a rake with rubber tines that won't tear up your perennials. A small hand rake really comes in handy for tight spots.

A heavy iron garden rake gets most of its use in the vegetable garden for leveling and smoothing after digging. I often turn the head upside down to get rid of dirt clods by beating them with it. I'm not kidding; it's the best way.

HOES

Not everyone needs a hoe. I use a standard type, mainly for making furrows for planting seeds of corn, beans, and other vegetables. I used to have an old hoe that must have been in the garage when I bought the house. Poorly designed and constructed, the blade would occasionally fly off the handle. I was doing some serious weeding one day, chopping out clumps of grass and clover, when the flying-off-the-handle episodes became more frequent and dangerous.

Few things in gardening cause as much cussing as a hose that kinks.

So get a quality hoe that will stay in one piece. Another hoe I use more frequently is the "action" or "shuffle" hoe, which has a thin sharp blade on a hollow head that shuffles back and forth, and which cuts small weeds off just below the soil surface.

HOSES AND GARDEN MISCELLANY

Even if you put in an automated underground irrigation system, you'll still need a hose. Few things in gardening cause as much cussing as a hose that kinks. You'll pay more for a quality hose, but, again, you'll keep your cool. Get one longer than you think you'll need. A 50' hose is shorter than you imagined.

Among the things I use on a constant basis are plastic spray bottles (for soap sprays), a plastic ten-gallon bucket for toting tools and collecting garden debris, a hose reel for quick roll-ups, and various hose attachments. For container gardening, I use a watering wand with an adjustable head that I can dial up to get everything from a fine mist to a powerful jet. It's similar to the one you may have in your shower that pulses and massages. The advantage is that you can get a delicate spray so that you don't wash away seedlings, or a more aggressive spray for washing down the patio and everything in between.

Among the tools I've yet to find a use for are the hand claw (I don't think my plants would want me disturbing their roots on a daily basis) and the bulb planter, an aluminum tube that would be better for taking geological core samples if it weren't guaranteed to bring on carpal tunnel syndrome within three minutes of use. Surely I've had a few others that have long been buried in the back corners of the potting shed.

Once your relatives and friends see that you've become a gardener, you're bound to get garden stuff as gifts. If they garden, perhaps they'll give you useful things like pots and tools. Try to steer them in the right direction so that they don't give you trinkets like pink flamingos and resin plaques that say "My Garden" or "Squirrel Crossing."

■ Start to Plant!

At some point you'll need to stop reading, quit planning, and go buy some plants. Get yourself to your local nursery. Ask for help. Try not to get distracted by every pretty flower you see. Follow your list just like at the grocery store. There are plenty of suggestions within the regional section of this book, which immediately follows this introduction.

Part of being a good gardener is being a good observer. Watch what happens in your garden through the seasons and learn from it. As your thumb starts to get a little green glow, branch out and try new things. If you do indeed kill a plant (and you will), figure out why. Plants want to live, so something went wrong. The answer is usually that the plant received too much or too little water. Always poke your finger in the soil several inches deep before you water. If it's moist, hold off.

You're off and running. Take some classes. Read some more books. Get dirty.

🌸 Section 2

Your Southern Garden

■ Ground Level

AMENDING SOIL

Whenever two gardeners get together, there are likely to be two, if not three, opinions expressed on any topic. In Rob Proctor's introduction to this book, he emphasized the importance of selecting plants that can grow in the soils of your area. While that approach makes good sense, it can limit the diversity of plants that will grow in difficult southern soils. My approach is different from Rob's—I do recommend amending your soil. As you cultivate your first garden, I expect that your approach will ultimately be somewhat different from either of ours.

In discussing soil amendment, at least two questions emerge: How come the weeds grow just fine in plain dirt, but the plants I want to grow don't? If I grow only native plants, can I avoid the hassle of amending the soil? The answer to both questions comes down to the nature of gardening. The very word, garden, has at its root the notion of guarding the cultivated space

Eye-catching gladiolas bloom well into summer from bulbs planted weekly, beginning in early spring. Stake at planting time to keep leaves and flowers clean.

around the house. Historically that space, often walled, sustained the family or community inside in times of pestilence, inclement weather, and war. When we garden, we take special care of the soil to keep it healthy and productive so we can grow a wide variety of plants in closer proximity to us than nature would allow in uncultivated soil. Even if they are all natives, the plants available wouldn't necessarily all grow in the same patch of land; but with our care, they can.

When you look at two gardens with similar plants and sunlight conditions in the same neighborhood, one often looks better than the other. The plants are stockier and greener, the flowers more abundant, the lawn invites your footstep, and the trees cast pleasing shade to cool the whole scene. Given equal investments of time and energy, the difference is most often the soil beneath the entire landscape. Anybody can have great soil; some of us just have to work harder at it than others. You improve the soil so it can sustain your plants to their maximum potential. In the long run, not only do they perform better, but you will be able to work less to care for them.

The key to soil improvement is to add organic matter in combinations that improve drainage conditions and create a capable rootzone. If soil amendment sounds like too much work, be prepared to plant, fertilize, and water more often if you want your garden to approach the good looks of the sumptuous one down the street.

It's up to the gardener to enable the soil ecosystem to host the finest roots on the block; fortunately, most of the work is on the front end.

Assessing Your Soil and Site

Native soils in the South run the gamut—some loamy, others clay-based, still others rather rocky, sandy, or silt-laden. But all are teeming with life. Because of the high level of microorganisms in these soils, they are called humid. Microorganisms use a lot of oxygen; so do plant roots. The gardener's job is to be sure both get what they need. As you get to know your property, there will likely be four kinds of soil. If you limit plant choices to those most naturally suited for the sort of soil that is present, only minimal soil amendment and regular cultivation will be needed. Knowing the composition of soils in your site and making a plan for the landscape gives you a good start.

Learn about the soils and spaces on your property with this exercise: take a sheet of paper and fold it in quarters. Open it back out and locate your house and other structures in their proper quadrant. Orient the drawing to see the path the sun takes across your property from sunrise to sunset. Next, draw in big trees, walls, and paths. Envision where water goes when it rains and draw arrows on the paper to show the flow. Now go out into the yard with the drawing and look around. Under the eaves (unless water runs there), between structures, and under large trees, the soil is dry and shady. At the crest, and along the street on the west and south sides, the soil tends to be dry and sunny. Damp areas may naturally occur or be created where you have installed irrigation or water regularly; these, too, are sunny or shady.

Drainage and Tilth

Unless you're planning a bog garden, it's a good idea to do a test for drainage before planting anything at a site new to you. Grab your shovel, sharpen it if you haven't recently, then dig a hole 12" deep and 12" across. Fill it with water and watch how the water drains. Soils that cannot hold the water for even 10 minutes, along with those that do not drain after as long as 45 minutes, need the most help in order to sustain a garden bed.

**Pink Country Girl mums and yellow coreopsis join silver lamb's ears
to create the exuberant mix of colors and flowers known as cottage garden style.**

Beyond being planted in well-drained soil, the challenge for many of our favorite plants, especially perennials, is to avoid root and crown damage in cold, wet, heavy soils and hot, dry ones. The roller coaster that is weather in our region can make soils wet one week and dusty the next, cold for a week and then warm for a month. Amending the soil so roots endure fewer rapid changes in their environment enables them to tolerate the extremes of our climate, summer and winter, and to produce plants that look good, grow well, and reward their gardener.

Organic matter is, by definition, anything that once was live, growing plant material, and that now has decomposed to one extent or another. The sources range from raked leaves in a pile behind the garage to ground bark, compost, peat moss, pinestraw, hay, and manure. Organic matter could be cited as a "miraculous soil additive," but no one variety corners the market. From leaf mold (the brown material you dig from that leaf pile after it has been sitting for a few months) to the cleanest peat harvest, all types of organic matter have the same basic ability to improve drainage and water-holding capacity when added to native soils.

Everything in soil, whether natural or added by you, consists of particles of varying sizes. As tiny as grains of sand look, the particles that form clay are much, much tinier. Ground peat

Clean gravel paths lead around and through a rustic structure reminiscent of old tobacco-drying sheds, where canna lilies and annual flowers bloom all summer.

and finely screened compost have larger particles than sand, chopped leaves and ground bark still larger, and so forth. Each of the larger particles of organic matter will bind to clay or sand when well mixed, creating larger spaces between clay particles and filling in the holes between sand grains. The result, perhaps ironically, is better drainage in clay and more water-holding capacity in sand.

It's all about improving the tilth, as the farmers say. Teach yourself about tilth with this quick test: grab a handful of soil and squeeze it. If the soil breaks up into dust or sticks to itself readily, its tilth is in trouble. Use this test on existing beds, ones you've improved, and any planting mixes you may consider buying for large projects. If, happily, that soil ball crumbles loosely through your fingers, you have achieved tilth and will be able to grow better plants, no matter what kind or combination you choose.

Step by Step

The following description of soil amendment is the prescription for preparing heavy soils for plants requiring excellent drainage. To grow plants that are less fussy in better-drained native soils, less amendment is necessary. The process of amending soil for a new bed to grow vegetables, flowers, or a hedgerow is essentially the same. Lay out the bed's design in your mind's eye, then create an edge around it with spray paint or string. Step back to see if the bed is big enough in proportion to the surrounding space and big enough to contain the numbers and sorts of plants you want to grow. When you're set on the site, use a flat-head shovel to scrape off any existing weeds or grasses from the space. Their nutritive value is negligible, but they can become troublesome weeds if dug into the bed. Next, dig a narrow ditch about 4" deep around the bed and toss what you dig into the bed.

Unless you love to wield a shovel, get a tiller for the next part of this job. Rentals are reasonable, or you can hire someone to dig to your specifications. First till or dig the native soil to a depth of 4" to 6", depending on what is physically possible in the bed. If you hit a hard spot at any depth, stop and build up soil on top of it instead of trying to dig further. Then pour organic matter, preferably a variety of different-sized particles, on top of the soil and begin tilling it in. Use a combination such as this one for a total of at least 4" of organic matter: ½" each of peat moss and manure (aged poultry manure is most nutritious, but cow or goat will do fine), 1" of compost, and 2" old leaves, gin moat, stable shavings, stump grindings, or ground bark. If you intend to plant right away, avoid fresh materials, which require several months to break down to usable condition. Add 1" of sand that is sharp, usually sold as masonry sand and noted for its jagged edges.

On top of all that, sprinkle garden or horticultural lime (not hydrated lime) and cottonseed meal (to feed the worms, who will further till the garden for you!). Literally sprinkle these across the whole bed, in a proportion like sugar on oatmeal before we started taking it plain. Finally, add elemental or complete fertilizers. These options are discussed in the section on fertilizer. Till

BLUE-RIBBON POTTED PLANTS

Fill large containers with big and boisterous plants like coleus, canna, and trailing sweet potato vine.

Big pots filled with wild mixes of perennials, annuals, and shrubs make bold statements on the deck, by the door, and out in the garden. Mix your own soil for container gardening to make watering less of a chore and perhaps save a dollar or two as well. Dump a big bag of potting soil into a wheelbarrow. (Choose a peat-based potting soil for best results.) Use that same bag to measure these ingredients: ½ bag ground bark, ½ bag compost, ¼ bag manure (unless you plan to put the containers inside!), and ¼ bag sharp sand. Sprinkle a light layer of garden lime and about the same amount of complete garden fertilizer over the pile of ingredients and mix well. Store in a covered plastic garbage can, if there's any left to store. With a mix this good, you'll just keep planting pots until it's used up. Quality ingredients in these proportions make it possible to grow just about anything in containers, including tomatoes, by watering and fertilizing regularly. By the way, a 30-gallon plastic garbage can of this mix makes an excellent birthday gift for any gardener! ∎

across the bed in each direction, then go diagonally, and finally straight across again. Rake until the mound of the bed gently slopes down to the ditch, like a big loaf of unsliced bread. In a short time, this pile will settle to a height of about 2" above ground level. If you have severe drainage problems and want to contain the mix in a raised bed, box it in with wood, bricks, or blocks instead of digging a ditch around it.

Renewing an existing bed or maintaining the one you've made can be a simple biseasonal routine. Mulch with organic matter that decomposes readily or can be removed and chopped up when its color or tendency to mat down around the plants becomes undesirable. Fast-rotting materials can be readily worked into the top 1" or 2" of the soil in most beds using a hoe or cultivator. Turn the old layer of mulch under in autumn, then add a fresh layer of mulch for winter protection. In spring, rake back the mulch around the plants and ring them with 1" of finely screened compost, then work it into the soil with a garden claw or similar tool.

Take it on faith that whatever organic matter you work into the soil will assist in building its structure and keeping it productive over a lifetime of gardening. Once you've created a successful bed, one that grows plants that are healthy and lush, you'll be a believer.

MULCHING

Mulch is essential for profitable gardening. Blanketing bare garden soil with 1" or 2" of mulch has several advantages, foremost that it goes a long way toward lowering maintenance time. Mulch suppresses weeds and improves conditions in the soil below it, thus boosting the growing environment for those all-important plant root systems. Soils neither get as soaked nor dry out as fast when mulch is in place. And if the mulch you use is organic, you can incorporate it in the steps described above to improve the soil.

Common organic mulches include straws (pine and wheat mostly), bark (pine and hardwoods), and leaf mold (the stage between raked leaves and compost). Leaf mold still has recognizable leaf shapes and pieces, but is dark brown and on its way to complete rot. Bark can be ground, shredded, or nugget-sized; choose among different kinds for looks and price, but don't forget the float factor. (The lighter materials can shift around in the bed or even drift out of it during heavy rains.) In most situations, 1" to 2" of mulch is adequate; using more can create a thickness that traps water intended for the plants and reduces air circulation in the bed. As a practical note, most professionals mulch the bed first, then install the plants. They say it saves time, and I say it keeps your pants cleaner since you're sitting or kneeling on fresh mulch, not soil.

Inorganic mulches, such as plastic sheeting, weed-barrier cloth, gravel, glass pebbles, and rocks have distinct and important uses, too. Gravel and rock mulches deliver colorful contrasts and, for those who like things neat, a tidy appearance to dry beds and areas planted with drought-tolerant plants (called "xeriscapes"). Sharp slopes and other difficult sites can benefit from weed-barrier cloth. The cloth makes it harder to renew the soil, since digging in the rotting mulch is not practical, but it is still possible to add compost around the plants in the spring. Black plastic mulch should be reserved for vegetable gardens, where it helps to warm the soil (useful for early planting). Both sheet materials should be laid out and buried at their edges to hold them in place. Then form holes for the plants by cutting Xs and folding the flaps back under the cover. Put a thin layer of straw or bark mulch on top of the weed-barrier cloth for looks and for preventing weeds in the planting areas, but leave black plastic uncovered for maximum soil-warming effect. To eliminate the weeds and many of their buried seeds in a new bed or a bed that has gone to seed, clear plastic can be tightly bound over these areas. Leave the sheath in place for at least six weeks in the summer to take advantage of the sun's heat and condensation, which will kill anything under the plastic.

COMPOSTING

The term "compost" has a host of definitions, how-tos, and what not to-dos, but understanding how organic matter rots, why and how to encourage it, and what to do with the results will make you a better gardener and citizen. If that sounds too good to be true, consider the alternative cycle of bag-and-buy. In the course of a year, trees drop leaves, annuals finish their season, lawns are mowed, and shrubs and perennials get cut back. Rural residents pile it all up and burn the debris, but city folk and suburbanites seldom have that option. Instead, they line the curb with bags to be picked up by the local garbage service and carted away, sometimes to municipal mulch piles, but more often to landfills. When you put the bags out at the curb instead of composting leaves and green matter, you let go of a superb resource, which you then must replace by purchasing organic matter and fertilizer! Home composting seldom provides enough of these materials for an entire garden, but when you put these leftovers to good use, the plants and your budget obviously benefit. Best of all, the landfill for which your taxes pay doesn't reach capacity so soon, and you can feel good knowing that simply by composting, you're taking responsible care of your own part of the world.

Here's how it works: Compost can range from piles of leaves (about 3' by 3' works well) dumped along the back of a garden border to organic matter contained in a series of open-air wood and wire enclosures. Self-contained compost bins are handy, so long as they are large enough to accommodate your garden's debris and don't hold water. Intact materials, like brown leaves and green grass clippings, decompose naturally over time in the presence of moisture and sunlight. That's it; you pile it up and it rots. This glorious process is accelerated by oxygen and by nitrogen, which encourage the essential digestive actions of microscopic organisms and earthworms.

If you exploit the factors in the composting process, the organic matter rots more quickly. Brown leaves alone will rot in six months to a year in the southern climate if you do nothing but pile them up. Toss in some green matter and a sprinkling of nitrogen fertilizer (like cotton-seed meal), turn it once a week, and monitor its water content and the process speeds up exponentially. To turn compost, just move the pile with a shovel or garden fork into a wheel-barrow if space is tight, into a second bin if you have one, or onto a tarp. Complete the process by returning the compost back into its place. Plenty of air will get into the mix as you move it, speeding the process along. Unless rainfall has been copious or nonexistent, it is seldom necessary to water a good heap. Compost that stays very wet needs more dry brown material; very dry piles need more green matter. As it's going along, bury eggshells, coffee grounds, and vegetable peelings for added nutrients in the finished product. The pile of leaves, grass, and other recognizable materials breaks down to become partially decomposed leaf mold and finally to arrive at the dark brown, moist state of compost. Good quality leaf mold makes an excellent mulch or soil amendment at almost any stage. Compost can be used as you dig it, or screened to a finer particle size for starting seeds or adding to potting mixes.

For superb contrast in a well-drained, sunny bed, choose spiky variegated yucca and softer, rounder Mexican bush sage, which displays purple flowers from summer into fall.

FERTILIZING

Imagine that somehow, by chance, a Martian surveyed a garden store full of fertilizer products, trying to interpret human behavior. It would seem from the amount of fine print we devote to the subject that every flower, tree, and soil type had nutrition needs as specific as the humans themselves. Turn that Martian loose among the pallets of lawn fertilizers, and the poor thing would surely believe we treasure turf beyond gold. For all that attention to chemical formulas, we are so obsessed with healthy greens that they must be a sacred resource. As a matter of fact, growing plants demand ample amounts of sunlight, water, and food. Period. How much sun and water plants need can be very specific, but which kind of fertilizer to use is open to debate. Thus, the array of products can be overwhelming to humans, let alone Martians!

Basically, we fertilize garden plants for the same reason we amend garden soils. That is, because we expect more of them than nature does, we want to keep them healthy and productive. In the early 1800s, a scientist considered insane by his colleagues proved that plant growth is influenced not only by sustenance from "earthly substances," those mysterious and unknowable essentials in soil, but also by chemicals. Once the others caught on, it still took a century to isolate all the elements found in plants: but at last, more than a dozen were identified. Green plants need carbon, oxygen, and hydrogen, but thanks to their abundance in nature, we don't have to supply them except in rare cases. They also need sulphur and calcium, both readily available in most soils. Other elements are needed, but three dominate the conversation, especially in the humid soils of our region.

The Big Three

Nitrogen (N) is essential to good green color, leaf size, and continuous growth. It is also the first soil element used up in the natural rotting process, and so must be made available to plants by the gardener. On fertilizer labels, numbers like "8-8-8" indicate the amount of nitrogen first, while phosphorus (P) and potassium (K) are indicated by the second and third numbers, respectively. Phosphorus gets bound up by southern soils and thus becomes unavailable to plant roots, so gardeners must apply it often enough to overcome the deficiency. Plants also need to get potassium through their roots; generally speaking it will be amply available in fertilizer combinations you're already applying. Both phosphorus and potassium are crucial to the development of long-lived stems, plentiful flowers, and strong cell walls in everything from roses to bell peppers. The other elements essential to plant growth are called trace elements because of the relatively minute quantities needed. The good news is that southern soils (especially clay) contain most of them; if not, most balanced fertilizers include the most important of them and supplemental drenches can be used.

The Point of It All

Building the garden that everyone talks about includes adding these essential elements as you amend and renew the soil. It is equally important to fertilize your plants during their growing season. Complete formula granular garden fertilizers contain the Big Three, but remember to examine those labels to find one with trace elements along with both fast- and slow-release action. The inclusion of these last two factors in the formula sets garden fertilizers apart from those better suited to agricultural uses (e.g., 13-13-13). Garden fertilizers are easier to incorporate into the soil and usually have more active ingredients per pound.

You can choose any brand of fertilizer that has the above-mentioned qualities, almost regardless of the arrangement of the numbers on the label. But do select one for the lawn (get one made for your type of turf) and a different one for beds with flowering plants and trees (10-30-15 is a common proportion). Popular houseplants can grow happily with only soluble fertilizers (those you mix in water), and gardeners with time to feed weekly nearly all year long do use them exclusively in the outdoor garden. That's more of a chore than most folks will do, so a combination of fertilizers is often more practical. Fertilizers can be balanced or specialized in their formulas (e.g., 20-20-20 or 16-28-18). If you use a specialized granular fertilizer such as 5-10-5, select a balanced soluble (20-20-20) to complement its formula.

If you select a specialty fertilizer for extensive plantings of particular plant groups, be specific. Formulas made for azaleas, hollies, and other acid-loving plants can be detrimental to other plants; rose foods can contain insecticides that are helpful for roses but unnecessary for other plants. (Indiscriminate use of insecticide reduces the number and effectiveness of beneficial insects in the garden. See the section on Troubleshooting below.) As you are tilling that new bed into shape, sprinkle a liberal amount of complete formula granular fertilizer over the bed and till it in before the final raking. (See "Basic Bags" sidebar for information on using individual elemental fertilizers in organic gardens.)

After the soil has been mixed and, ideally, allowed to rest for a month or more before planting, the routines of fertilizing and watering sustain your plants. Healthy, container-grown plants with plenty of white roots need only be watered in well after planting in good garden soil. When transplanting them from one place in the garden to another, or planting distressed plants of any sort, water in with fertilizer. Half-strength soluble fertilizer, fish emulsion, compost tea, or a root-stimulator formula can help prevent transplant shock in such difficult situations.

Doing It Right

Here's the bottom line on water and fertilizer application: do it. As a rule of thumb, don't let leaves wilt or get pale during the growing season. Beyond these hard rules, deciding when and how to water and fertilize is mostly a matter of finesse. Most plants will grow a little or at least maintain their progress with less water and fertilizer than most gardeners provide. As the landscape matures, if you renew the soil each season, annual applications may be all that is necessary to maintain trees, shrubs, and even lawns. But if you are trying to get an important hedge to fill in, grow a bountiful flower and vegetable garden, or keep the lawn healthy despite foot traffic, consistency is the key. If your primary granular fertilizer bag says to reapply after three months, use a bit less than the recommended amount a few weeks sooner or use a soluble formula mixed in water between granular applications. The idea here is to grow what are called "thrifty" plants by keeping nutrients available as the plants require them without fluctuations.

Growing a bold planting of annual flowers or delicious vegetables means watering and fertilizing routinely for nearly constant effect. Other plant groups make fewer demands; they will be outlined below. To keep the heavy feeders happy, start with amended soil, water in with a half-strength soluble formula, and repeat in a week. Apply granular food by using a hoe to cut a shallow line alongside or around the plants and put fertilizer in it, then re-cover with soil. Continue through the season with at least two soluble applications a month. Remembering to feed the plants will get you out into the garden a bit longer so you can keep an eye out for bugs and buds. One of the best feelings in the world is to sit on the edge of the sprinkler's

---

BASIC BAGS

A host of fertilizer products await, hoping that someone will find them fascinating and take them home. Here, without fanfare, are a few translations of what those complicated names mean. Elemental fertilizers provide nutrients one at a time. Many are derived from living sources and thus are favored by organic gardeners. Everyone else can enjoy the benefits of these fertilizers as well. Examples include:

- Nitrogen: Nitrate of soda, cottonseed meal, blood meal
- Phosphorus: ground phosphate rock, superphosphate
- Potassium: wood ash, muriate of potash
- Aluminum sulfate: used to alter soil chemistry to keep hydrangeas blue
- Iron: used to reduce the incidence of leaf yellowing between the veins (chlorosis) ■

Let the shade of azaleas shelter woods hyacinths for a stunning spring scene.
Both plants can benefit from the same fertilizers made for acid-lovers.

spray, cooling off after making the rounds with fertilizer mixed in a watering can. The best part is that the plants look better immediately, and who doesn't like instant gratification?

Most perennial flowers and shrub roses can be fed slightly less often than the annuals. When new growth begins in the spring, spread compost around their base and work in granular fertilizer according to their girth as directed on the label. As the flowers bloom, fertilize again with a granular formula if you want to encourage growth. After each flush of flowers, feed the plants

Simplify caring for annuals by combining them. Colorful leaves of perilla and Joseph's coat stand out against bold purple fountain grass in bloom for months.

with a soluble fertilizer mixed in water. Lawns, shrubs, and trees still in the active growing phase of their lives appreciate granular formulas in spring (usually after flowering) and summer. If they are not performing as well as you'd like, add a fall fertilizing, but be sure it is a specialty formula made for use in autumn or one containing no nitrogen at all (such as 0-10-10). If nitrogen is provided in the fall, it will do its job of encouraging leafy new growth, which is very vulnerable to winter damage.

Wet Schemes

The role of water in how fertilizer works cannot be understated; the grainy mix cannot transform into a solution plants can use without being dissolved into the soil by water. Likewise, plants cannot take up nutrients if they are wilted; the attempt can actually burn their roots. If you have (accidentally, of course) allowed plants to wilt, water them and allow them to recover before fertilizing. The subject of when to water is much debated, but it comes down to this: apply water slowly, allowing it to soak into the rootzone. This way of watering encourages deep root systems for plants that are more physically stable and drought-resistant in the long run. Water often enough to prevent soil from crusting or plants from wilting.

■ Design Choices

Whether you begin with a former cow pasture that is flat, sunny, and treeless, or "inherit" a property full of green delights, garden design is all in the way you bring the elements together. Common to everything designed, from furniture to flower arrangements to park-sized gardens, are the concepts of line, color, and form. Lines lead your eye to one place and not another; color defines and accents; and form literally shapes the landscape.

LINES COMMUNICATE TONE

Formal gardens tend to have strong lines and often plenty of right angles. Any visitor knows immediately where to go and how to get there because the lines guide both eyes and feet. Formal plantings are neatly groomed, often with careful attention to pruning and seasonal color successions. The joy of a formal garden or planting is its comfortable predictability and reliable strong design. Those carefully edged beds and clipped shrubs, roses in a raised brick bed, and neat paths between features make people of all ages feel welcome. Here's a secret no gardener will admit, but many use: if you keep the edging plants clipped and the paths clear, the plants within a formally defined bed can be a bit wild and still look more than presentable. And when splashes of colorful annuals or a host of daylilies are surrounded by neat border of grass or dwarf holly, they truly look like the stars they are meant to be.

By contrast, informal or naturalistic garden style often features lines that bend gently and may lead to a destination or simply to another curve on the way to someplace as yet unrevealed. The casual visitor may not immediately know where to sit, or how many "surprises" await. Naturalistic landscapes are intentionally less regimented in design, plant choices, and mood;

WHAT ELSE IS ON THAT SHELF?

Specialty fertilizers offer formulas for everything from African violets to fruit trees, with more ways to deliver the goods than I can count. They also provide convenience and plant-specific nutrition. If you become obsessed with a particular plant group, buy the food meant for it, such as bulb food for the daffodil. If orchids are your thing, or fig trees, and you have a lot of them, keep a fertilizer made for them on hand.

Spikes, tablets or slow-release pellets, and constant feed reservoirs are worth exploring because they simply make some routine tasks easier to do.

Spikes make it simple to locate fertilizer at the drip line of trees without overfeeding the lawn beneath. Slow-release pellets make it easy to limit houseplants to a desired size; to continue regularly feeding with soluble fertilizers will make them continue to grow. To maintain their good health and color, use only slow-release pellets in their pots; the fertilizer is released when you water, and that's plenty. Reservoir pots with wicks make it simple to feed plants like African violets that thrive when nutrients are constantly present in water so that they can take them up on demand. If it saves you time and gives the plants what they want, I'm all for it. ■

**LEFT: Daffodils carpet the way to a formal gazebo in spring, then give way to annuals all summer.
RIGHT: Hyacinth beans pour from the arch in an informal planting.**

rectangular beds may sit opposite round ones, or borders may feature unpruned sasanqua and wildly sprouting silverberry as a background. The edges of naturalistic plantings are often more suggested than clearly defined, with ornamental grasses and Country Girl mums spilling out exuberantly. Informal designs can accommodate a variety of materials in paths and a wide range of textures and ornamental elements. Collections of wind chimes and yard art may overwhelm or seem out of place in a formal garden, but any sort of personal whimsy can easily find a place in looser, more informal designs.

THE POWER OF COLOR

Color is a moody thing; after all, most people feel more somber in a gray suit than in red running clothes no matter what they're doing that day. Gardens painted in pastels invite you to linger, like the muted tones in a fine restaurant. But fill the same space with primary reds and yellows and not only does everything seem to speed up, you'll swear the temperature is a few degrees higher, too. Depending on what year it is, garden experts tout a rainbow of colors or monochromatic plant palettes. As you find colors and combinations that please you, remember that the words "eclectic style" describe everything except what's trendy, just in case your choices cannot be found in the latest magazine articles.

In addition to warming up the environment, red and yellow call attention to themselves and their space. A baker's rack full of potted red geraniums by the front door is as effective as a big welcome sign: "Enter here, World." Spread yellow flowers among any other colors in annual and perennial groups to make pinks, blues, and whites stand out in contrast. Pinks and lavenders work to soften the scene, and blue calms it even more. But don't leave out the yellow and white, even gold and amber, in your garden color scheme. Especially if evenings are prime time for garden sitting in your busy household, plant lots of blue and white with dashes of pink and yellow. As the day fades to twilight, it takes a lot of blue to keep up with the sunset tones, but it's well worth the effort to include it. White can take over after nightfall, as easily as moonflowers in summer and white tulips and daffodils in winter. White calls you out into the night garden, especially if it is illuminated by the moon or a lighting system.

In the deepest shade gardens, planting a range of green hues will both brighten and add depth to beds under trees. The addition of an understory tree to such settings, whether a red maple or white-flowered camellia, provides a stunning focal point, thanks to its color. Flowers

To keep your favorite, or signature, color in the garden all year, use it in lawn furniture and hardscape, then repeat that color in plants—such as banana and amaranth in this setting.

Palms lend just enough shade for this glowing combination of plants. Bromeliad, lantana, and coleus work together to bring out each other's gold and copper hues.

and leaves are usually the primary source of color in the garden, but architectural pieces, or "hardscape," can add or reinforce hues you want to emphasize. A brilliant landscape architect always makes sure a client's favorite color can be seen in the garden year-round. If blue tops your list, plant cornflowers and blue pansies for fall and spring, and blue salvias for summer and fall. But be sure to paint a wooden chair, or a swing, or even a bird feeding station in that same beloved signature shade for continuity and sheer pleasure. On a gray day in January, that blue chair will shine to remind you of what is soon to come.

THE 3-D GARDEN

Form brings the third dimension to garden design with the density and silhouettes of plants, hardscape, and architecture on the site. Think of the central point of your back garden, the place to which the lines lead you when you look out the back window or stand at the back door. Envision a glider there, with roses climbing over its top. Its form, a basic rectangle, might be a bit stark against a wood fence or standing alone in the lawn. But add the rounded shapes and arching lines of the climbing rose and the effect is a dynamic form with three-dimensional appeal.

Form can work to highlight a garden space or conceal it. A neatly sheared evergreen hedge has a boxy form and sets off whatever is in front of it or inside its perimeter, a living picture

**A clipped hedge makes the perfect backdrop to a delightful hodgepodge,
including spider flowers, salvia, and pink dahlias, and lends silent order to the scene.**

frame for you to fill. Put that boxy form out in an open area (think of a huge shrub, big trellis, or a group of trees out in the middle of the lawn) and it becomes the focus instead of the frame. Let a path lead around that form to create a surprise space in the garden. A water feature, a bench (cornflower blue, perhaps), or a special plant only visible behind that form gives it another role, that of screen or garden room divider. Common forms besides the box shape are mounds, vase shapes, and pyramidal or cone shapes. Each can be employed alone or in groups to establish rhythm in the design, lend perspective to the other elements, and put the garden in proper proportion, or scale, to the house and other structures.

An important design consideration for many gardeners is shade. Its power to shelter and create cool microclimates grants a few more hours of prime time. As one of my garden mentors showed me around her shady garden, she mentioned, "I can work in the yard at high noon in July; can you?" Get to know the three kinds of shade; you'll love them all. When high shade falls under a tall tree canopy, garden lighting conditions are terrific. If you can read a newspaper in that shade, you can grow most flowers and many vegetables as well as shrubs. In fact, the annuals commonly labeled "sun or part shade" are at their best here. A totally different environment is dappled shade. Sun shines in spots for all or part of the day; shade moves through the area with the sun's daily path. Some parts of this environment are shady all day, but others have plenty of light for flowering plants. Take a day off and watch how the sun changes during the

With a simple fence to divide it from the pasture beyond, this graceful border offers red, white, and several shades of pink in gladiolas, pansies, and wine cup.

day to find the sunny spots and shady nooks. Last, if no direct sunlight makes its way into the space, and reflected and indirect light are the only sources, make room for every shade of green for color and texture. Use mulches, rocks, and lightly colored hardscape to brighten the scene and add light-reflecting surfaces.

DESIGNING FOR YOUR LIFESTYLE

In defining your style, and thus the design of your garden, it's important to know how much maintenance it will demand and how you can provide it. Notice I didn't say, "how you can accomplish it," since no one is bound by any oath to personally execute every task. If you've never taken care of your own yard, try everything from digging to deadheading until you (and the other budding gardeners at your house) can decide what you hate to do. If mowing and tilling wears you out, hire the neighborhood teenager earning his or her way to college. Perhaps you have a phobia about pruning; if so, no doubt there's a professional nearby who will do it or teach you how for a reasonable fee. You may be surprised how soothing it can be to weed a flowerbed, or it may make you crazy. Another pair of eyes and hands can be helpful, but that "honey-do" list has its civil limits, even in the garden.

Each design decision brings its own set of maintenance requirements. For example, growing mostly lawn may entail several hours weekly to mow and edge, but can make any size garden space seem larger than it is. If you like a broad view, more park-like and kid-friendly, grow more lawn. Where flowerbeds and borders surround it, the lawn is not only physically smaller, but the space immediately feels more intimate. Its maintenance will be less routine after planting and likely less time-consuming on a weekly basis for the same size area.

Arranging the Space

The same principle applies when designing flowerbeds or borders; size matters and can affect maintenance. Envision a backyard space, a regular shape slightly wider than it is deep. For maximum growing space for plenty of annuals, perennials, and shrubs, a border along three sides of that space seems logical. The feature that defines a border is its backdrop and the fact that it is not intended to be viewed from all sides; that is, it has a front, side, and back. However, keeping after the weeds, deadheading the flowers, and clipping the shrubs takes several hours a week for much of the year, and such a large border may mean less lawn than you would like. Consider a flowerbed, instead. Its defined space is meant to be seen from all sides, so it can contain plenty of flowers per square foot with lawn on three or four sides. Its impact on the landscape will be just as great as the more complicated border, but less tedious to maintain.

For a less closed-in feeling, create an island or kidney-shaped bed at the center of the lawn area where people and breezes circulate freely. Or, locate that bed off to one side to soften the symmetry of the yard and lend a more casual style to the landscape. For an always lovely bed, place focal point shrubs at the center and fill the spaces on all sides with sections or swaths of plants, flowers, or even vegetables and herbs. An especially charming combination for a bed 12' long and 8' wide includes a trio of fringe flowers flanked by maiden grass. This natural division of the bed into front and back views offers space for annual flowers, bulbs, daylilies, and iris to be seen from the house. But go around to the other side to pick tomatoes, basil, bush beans, and squash.

ENCOURAGING WHIMSY—AND GARDENERS

I am not the least bit above bribery when it comes to getting my children into gardening. In fact, I've made it a policy always to accept every unrecognizable ornament, bowl, and geegaw they created in school or at camp, then use it to get the kids into the garden. I make a big deal of placing whatever it is in the garden, in a "special" place where it can be appreciated (occasionally, I'll admit, I pick a less conspicuous spot for some of the stranger pieces) and doesn't have to be dusted (yippee!). Sometimes one of the kids will pull a weed obscuring the view of a plate made by pressing a six-year-old's hand into plaster, or tell me that he or she wants to put more tulips in the bed with that address plate carved out of wet mud at age ten. I figure it works, since they notice what's out in the garden! Early on in their gift-buying career, I steered them to wind chimes and gardenesque jewelry. The result has been an ongoing collection of Mother's Days and birthdays with increasingly unusual wind chimes in bamboo, bone, brass, thin metal pansies, and thick metal tubes; some that clank (made from old forks and spoons) and some that are positively enchanting in their harmonies. They all have a story and I treasure them. I was especially tickled when, after giving me enough watering can pins and garden tool earrings to last a lifetime, they turned to squirrels, armadillos, and other odd critters. They give them to me because they've seen them in our garden. Over the years I have tried everything to get my children interested in gardening so that someday, at the very least, they'll call me when they realize the azaleas have overtaken the windows of their new home. Hopefully, they'll say, "Mama, what time of year do you prune those shrubs that bloom every spring?" and I'll know the lessons stuck a little bit. ∎

LEFT: Naked ladies win a prominent place in this group when they emerge, leafless, in summer.
RIGHT: White flowers of hostas and impatiens brighten this shady nook, and lead both eyes and feet along the path.

Public Spaces

Traditional front yard plantings usually feature a tree or two, some shrubs skirting the house, and maybe a flowerbed along the sidewalk or between it and the garage. These spaces are defined by the architecture of the abode, and are natural places for plants to soften the abrupt lines where the structure meets the ground. Usually the plantings are shrubs and trees, durable and lovely, chosen for their year-round good looks and forgiving nature. If you go on vacation, or forget to water or prune, a well-designed foundation planting will not embarrass you. Take the next step and customize it to lend your style to traditional formal designs. Add a climbing plant to a pillar or post, or add shrub roses to that row of azaleas across the front porch. Blanket the ground by the sidewalk with daylilies and daffodils amid the lily turf. Creating a distinctive front garden need not add hours of work each month, but can set your home apart as effectively as painting the front door bright pink.

The Wild Outback

Often the back garden is where you experiment with more time-consuming designs, where you can comfortably curve a path around the patio to the pond and screen the air-conditioning equipment at the same time. This is where you can plant perennials at will or dig them up, without leaving holes in the view while you decide what will grow better in that spot. When you want to grow a tree everyone says won't grow, or a tomato plant in a garbage can, it's a big decision to put it front and center; but a spot in the back garden is much less intimidating. Feeling less exposed, you can wait a couple of years for the hosta to spread, or the native plant to come into its own when they're planted in the less public parts of your garden. The maintenance in such a space can be spread out over a couple of hours a week for most of the year and its rhythm can readily match your pace.

In designing a less formal, more personal garden space, remember that curves and repetition are soothing and will unify even a strangely diverse plant collection. Sketch out where you want the beds to be, and even if their back edges are necessarily straight, lay out a series of broad curves to lead your eye around the garden. Then select three to five places in the beds for evergreen shrubs or trees to provide comforting visual stability. Repeat the broad curve and use no more than two or three different anchor plants (those evergreens) and the scene will be coherent, no matter what else you decide to grow.

Anchors and Guides

Every garden style needs hardscape to keep it from floating in space visually and to provide constancy as the seasons change. Anything permanent in the landscape is referred to as the garden's "bones," and many of those pieces are hardscape. Evergreen plants maintained at a particular height and shape, and large trees (even those that lose their leaves), can be bones, but are not hardscape because they are alive. Here are the most common hardscape elements: structures (including your house), fences, gates, paths, water features, boulders, rock-lined stream beds, gazebos, arbors, trellises, along with (if they are permanently located) containers, statues, swings, gliders, furniture, and yard art. To be well anchored, few gardens need all of them.

Take it from one who knows: hardscape is not meant for impulse shopping. Look before you leap into huge pieces for small gardens or vice versa. Proportion, the heart of a pleasing

LIGHT UP THE NIGHT

Close the drapes at dusk and you'll miss half the show your garden offers. The night garden will draw you out to hear the crickets, have a meal, and smell the flowers—if you add some lighting to the scene. Two major types of garden lighting are used, and both have advantages.

LOW VOLTAGE LIGHTING. For less money than you might think, a low-voltage lighting system can give you the freedom to light trees for dramatic silhouettes and illuminate decks around pools and garden paths to seating areas and benches. Security lights can be part of the system and attached to motion sensors. Low volts are a permanent installation, with their wires buried neatly below ground and their operating controls always within your reach. The disruption they cause is minimal when compared to your ability to light each section on demand.

SOLAR LIGHTING. The advantage of a solar lighting system is its versatility and ease of add-on installation. A line of solars between the driveway and the front door will come on daily to light the footpath; similarly, the lamps can line a bed to set it off, or rest in planters by the patio to set the mood for dining. You can put a few lights in and add more without digging up the lawn. Solar lights do not use electricity, but are generally of lower wattage than low-volt systems and, of course, are completely dependent on sunny days to make them work. ∎

design, means that a garden home backyard isn't the place for a gazebo that seats twelve people. That sheltered seating can be yours (though maybe only for four) in a wire arbor with seats, or two benches and a table, without overwhelming the space. The opposite poor use of proportion is illustrated by a ride through too many otherwise lovely suburban neighborhoods. Two- or three-story houses, often on small lots, offer nothing taller or stronger than a pair of planters flanking the front door, dwarfed by the house. Step out from the house into the sunny front yard and install two tall stone columns or a wide wooden pergola to support roses or perennial vines. The immediate effect is to bring the landscape into proportion with the house and beautify its starkly upright form by giving it "feet."

Practical Beauties

Think twice about the trellises you choose: some are downright cute but hopelessly inadequate for our region's vigorous vines, which require constant pruning. If you want to prune constantly, try bonsai. Coral honeysuckle, moonflower, wisteria, and hyacinth bean will quickly cover a 4' wire obelisk and head for whatever else is nearby. Elevate short trellises by putting cement blocks under them or attaching their legs to pipe extensions. Make the most of vertical gardening possibilities by choosing durable trellis materials that are attractive when not covered by leaves. If you paint them, use your signature color for even greater harmony and continuity. Their material, and that of all forms of hardscape, goes a long way toward setting the mood in your garden, be it friendly, humorous, or even awe-inspiring. Pressure-treated wood structures (benches, decks, or arbors) offer a naturally casual look, but can be lathed, sculpted, and painted into formal baroque or gingerbread pieces. Likewise, a set of library lions at the garden entrance with a stone fence and gate sends a decidedly different message than a hogwire fence and gate covered with morning glories. Though both are hardscape with the same function of defining space, the first challenges you to enter, while the second soothes your senses and draws you near.

WATER IN THE GARDEN

For a minute, think of why you like going to the beach. If it's all about the sound of water, you're up for adding a water feature to your garden. It may not be crashing waves, but the sound of water falling and flowing changes everything. Water muffles the world and gives you something to focus on, to relax and enjoy just being for a moment, or more. The sight of serene water, whether a whiskey barrel with a bamboo gravity fountain, a fish pond, or a reflecting pool, inspires and calms your mood, day or night. Add night lighting, some fish, and nocturnal lilies, and invite the frogs over to create a feature with more entertainment than any floor show.

When you're ready, start your water gardening experience with these tips from veterans:

1. Most gardeners complain their first water garden is too small, so make yours a little larger than you think is adequate.
2. Go with the natural flow in choosing a site; it's just not natural for a pond to be at the top of the garden nor where the water runs through constantly.
3. Half a day of sun on the water helps keep it in balance and slows down algae growth.
4. Put the water feature in view of your house, but locate it with seating on the far side, too, for an additional, more secluded view.
5. Be sure to include plants with sword-shaped leaves that reach for the sky. In classic water garden designs, the eye goes from the chaos of the world below to the serenity of the water and then upward to the sky for inspiration. ■

Hear the calming sounds of this water feature, then see the sweet sculpture on its ledge.
Elephant ears make a perfect frame for this focal point.

Using hardscape as a focal point in garden design also requires a healthy dose of self-exami-
nation. You're going to live with these pieces longer than your living room furniture, probably,
so go for passion over utility. Boulders for a waterfall, bridges, sculptures, or architectural pieces
like mantles and columns can transform a simple scene into a memorable one. Place them where
sight lines converge naturally when seen from an Adirondack chair in a serene spot, or at the
head of a rectangular bed or pond to create a focal point. Group small sculptures together in

a grotto of ferns or place one large piece at the center of a bed of monkey grass. Use hardscape to direct traffic, as in a series of planters along the driveway. Let it dominate the view from the house, the gate, or the street. Make it a destination, like a fountain that leads you across a garden to smell the roses planted around it. Create a surprise in the garden: a simple mantle placed between two trees is visible in winter, but only apparent in the summer garden from inside the wooded area.

Design, and sometimes redesign, is all about the gardener's satisfaction, making the garden a pleasure to see and not too much of a pain to maintain. A gardener invited me over to see her new landscape, a stark line of windmill palms echoing the perfect rectangle of the backyard pool. The palms rested in beds of mulch with dramatic lighting at their bases. Then she walked me around the side of the house where a wildly undulating perennial border leaped and surged with colorful flowers. The perennials had been in view of the pool, until she realized their exuberant cottage style ruined the mood of a relaxing time spent playing in the water. Every spent flower or new weed caught her eye and demanded care, so she moved them. The palms' cleanly upright lines have the opposite effect: if they demand at all, it is that you float aimlessly and gaze at their dramatic fronds silhouetted against the sky. Effectively combining gardening into your personal lifestyle makes for a long-lived and enriching experience.

■ Plants for Success

To give you the best chance of success in growing your new garden in the South, I am listing 50 plants that are most likely to succeed in USDA zones 7, 8, and 9, as shown on the map at the beginning of this book. You'll notice that for each plant, I'm giving you basic information on the category of plant (for example, perennial, tree, or annual), the way in which it can be used (a good shade plant, a great plant for sunny borders), the kind of soil in which the plant will grow best, its zone hardiness, and the mature size of the plant (to prevent you from planting something that will outgrow its space—or, just as important, to help you choose plants that will fill in an area well). Most of your local nurseries will carry these 50 popular plants. There's lots of variety in color, texture, form, and category of plant within this list. But, of course, the joy of gardening is to make your own discoveries. Growing these plants will give you the confidence to expand your gardening horizons!

SOIL SMARTS TO PREVENT PLANT PROBLEMS

In the plant descriptions in this book, three terms are used to describe the optimum soil conditions for that plant. Mostly they tell you what kind of drainage to provide, as measured by the amount of amending indicated. The term "well-drained" refers to native soil that has good drainage or has been amended with 1" or 2" of leaf mold and sand. "Organic" means native soil plus two or three different forms of organic matter. And "fertile" indicates additions of organic matter and a complete granular fertilizer. You'll find most of the plants in this book need good drainage and will perform best with the other elements included.■

PERENNIALS

PLANTAIN LILY
Hosta spp.
Category: shade perennial
Use: for color and texture in shade, flower spikes in summer
Soil: organic, consistently moist, well-drained
Hardiness: zones 3–9
Mature size: 12" to 40"

Wider than they are tall, hostas send out an oversized mat of colorful leaves in spring, followed by tall flower spikes in summer. Their popularity in our region is well-deserved; once established, hostas never miss a beat in hot, humid conditions. Standards include 'Paul's Glory' and 'Guacamole', but some have intriguing names, such as 'Elvis Lives' or 'Feather Boa'. Look for slug-resistant varieties like 'Sum and Substance', 'Big Daddy', and 'Fragrant Blue'.

Plantain lily (*Hosta* spp.)

Hostas thrive in light, dappled, or full shade and well-drained, organic, fertile soil. Plant them with compatible bed partners like swamp spider lilies, red spider lilies, and daffodils for nearly year-round color in a shady spot. Dig a hole wider than the container the hosta was growing in, and slightly deeper, then install the plant so its crown is slightly above ground level. Water in very well and blanket with any organic mulch.

Fertilize hostas regularly with a complete garden formula during the growing season. Do not allow them to dry out. Turn under the mulch as it rots and replace it annually when you clean up the clumps after the first frost. Wait until the clumps are well established, usually three years, before dividing or moving hostas.

When choosing hostas, bear in mind that blue-leaved varieties are generally less heat- and sun-tolerant than those with green leaves, and that solid-colored leaves usually adapt to more shade than bicolored. Gulf Coast gardeners should grow hostas in deeper shade than do gardeners in other parts of the Southeast, with more attention to consistent soil moisture.

Potential problems: slugs, snails, voles, and deer are common pests.

SHASTA DAISY
Leucanthemum x *superbum*
Category: sun to light shade (coastal areas) perennial
Use: line sidewalks or create accents and borders in spring and summer flower beds
Soil: very well-drained, fertile
Hardiness: zones 6–9
Mature size: 12" to 3'

Shasta daisies have been grown in our region for more than a century, beloved for their classic yellow centers and white petals. Bushy green clumps send up strong stems topped with single or double flowers. Popular selections of Shasta daisy include 'Becky' (large flowers, strong stems), 'Little Miss Muffett' (single flowers, 12' tall plants) and 'Alaska' (single flowers on big plants that tolerate cold weather well). Fancier, but as easy to grow, are standard-sized, double-flowered Shasta daisies 'Marconi' and 'Esther Read'.

Plant daisy clumps in fall or spring in very well-drained soil. Space plants 8" to 12" apart, depending on the mature size of your selection. Water in well and spread a blanket of organic mulch around each clump, but do not cover the crown. Shasta daisies also grow easily from seeds planted in small pots in spring or fall and transplanted to the garden when 4" tall.

Fertilize Shasta daisy clumps in early spring with a granular flower formula and repeat when flower buds appear. Turn under mulch that has begun to rot, and replace the mulch annually. If your soil is heavy or not as well drained, dig the daisies up each year, then divide and replant them. In better soil conditions, daisies should be divided every three years to keep the flowers coming.

If you have a larger or consistently damper site, grow the native 'Oxeye' daisy. But give it room; this one spreads by rhizomes underground, and reseeds itself too.

Potential problems: gall disease can split crowns; if this happens, dispose of the plants.

Shasta daisy (*Leucanthemum* x *superbum*)

GIANT CONEFLOWER
Rudbeckia maxima
Category: sun perennial
Use: for borders of summer garden beds
Soil: any well-drained soil
Hardiness: zones 7–9
Mature size: 6' to 8' in bloom

When it comes to perennials for the sunny garden, giant coneflowers are as dependable as your favorite pair of jeans. Dressed up or dressed down, they look good with little maintenance. With eye-catching daisy-shaped flowers and bright gold petals with rich brown, very prominent seed-bearing cones jutting out of their center, the giant coneflowers, like their relatives the black-eyed Susans, are easy to grow and surprisingly dramatic.

Planted as a summer hedge, the bluish-green leaves of giant coneflower whirl around strong stems. Reliably reaching 7' tall in full bloom, they come back thicker and stronger every year. But grown in an island bed among wildly striped ornamental grasses and spiky purple-blue salvias, the black-eyed Susan's giant cousin softens the design with its distinct, sophisticated profile.

Any well-drained fertile soil will do for giant coneflowers, but tightly packed clays should be amended with organic matter to improve their structure. Space giant coneflower plants 2' to 3' apart; they will fill it rapidly. Keep the plants moist with regular watering and a layer of organic mulch. In subsequent years, you may take root cuttings of mature plants and replant them in good garden soil. Fertilize each spring when new growth begins, and again in midsummer if the season has been very rainy. Cut down old flower stalks after the first frost.

For an excellent native, reseeding *Rudbeckia*, consider classic black-eyed Susan (*R. hirta*).

Potential problems: few pests ever trouble this plant family.

LOUISIANA IRIS
Iris hybrid
Category: sun or light shade native perennial
Use: in beds, bogs; around and in water features for late spring bloom
Soil: consistently moist, very organic soil
Hardiness: lower zones 6–9
Mature size: 3'

Hybridized from four swamp iris natives, Louisiana irises are a hardy, colorful bunch, and easier to grow throughout our region than most other irises. These irises have sharply pointed, stiffly upright leaves and flowers ranging from 3" to 7" across in every shade of red, blue, white, yellow, and purple. Enjoy them outdoors; their aroma is pungent in the vase. Classic varieties include 'Marie Caillet' (purple with yellow "eyes"), 'Colorific' (purple with white center petals), 'Old South' (light-streaked yellow), 'Koorawatha' (golden yellow), 'Cherry Bounce' (pure red), and 'Anne Chowning' (dark red with yellow "eyes").

ABOVE: Black-eyed Susan (*Rudbeckia hirta*)
BELOW: Louisiana iris (*Iris* hybrid)

Daylily (*Hemerocallis* 'Stella d'Oro')

Unlike other irises, these begin growing in the fall, so they can be dug, divided, and replanted in late summer. Choose sunny areas, except on the Gulf Coast, where light shade is preferred. Plant rhizomes 1" deep and at least 12" apart in soil rich in organic matter, but do not add lime or bone meal. Keep Louisiana irises moist while they are growing, from when the new leaves emerge until after the flowers finish and the leaves die back the next year. In late winter, use fertilizer made for azaleas and camellias and an organic mulch that is ground or shredded rather than pinestraw in this damp setting. Cut down stems as the flowers fade, but wait to remove leaves until they go dormant in summer.

Other reliable irises are the tall yellow flag (*I. pseudocorus*), blue flag (*I. versicolor*), southern blue flag (*I. virginica*) and hybrid Siberian irises

Potential problems: few pests, but for slugs and snails, sprinkle diatomaceous earth around clumps. If leaves develop spots, remove them; spray new growth with fungicide.

DAYLILY
Hemerocallis spp.
Category: full sun or light shade perennial
Use: in beds and borders for spring and summer blooms
Soil: well-drained, organic
Hardiness: zones 6–9
Mature size: 18" to 3'

Daylily season lasts for months. Though each blossom lasts just one day, there can be a dozen in succession on each plant. Daylilies can be enjoyed as individuals, lined up along front edges of large perennial borders filled with iris, salvia, and giant coneflowers, or in masses filling colorful beds.

The most popular daylilies are hybrids, but older types remain garden standards. Some lose all their leaves each year, others lose some, and still others are evergreen. Consult local daylily societies and nurseries for well-adapted varieties for your area. Across the South, 'Stella d'Oro' is everywhere, from botanical gardens to restaurant parking lots. This variety makes neat clumps, blooms repeatedly, and is nearly pest-free. Its yellow flowers harken back to the classic 'Lemon Daylily', early- and once-blooming, fragrant, and still available.

Plant the old favorites en masse, separate from less aggressive, fancy-flowered hybrids. Prepare a well-drained native soil, amended if necessary with 2" worth of organic matter to improve drainage. Space plants 12" apart, and do not bury the crown.

Snap off aging flowers to encourage more, and cut off stems and seedpods to nurture the clump. Keep mulch to a minimum and soak the soil weekly during dry spells. After two or three years, crowded plants should be dug up and divided, then replanted in soil freshly amended with 2" of organic matter. Extend the daylily bed, make a new one, or pot up the extras for a plant swap.

Potential problems: streaked or spotted leaves; remove them and spray new growth with fungicide; then dig and divide plants that do not bloom.

ROSE VERBENA
Verbena canadensis
Category: sun perennial
Use: spilling from beds and containers spring and summer
Soil: well-drained, organic, fertile
Hardiness: zones 6–9
Mature size: 10" to 12" tall and spreading

Rose verbena plants trail fuzzy green leaves and blooms on every stem. Though called 'rose', this type of verbena covers the spectrum of colors, except for yellow. Newer varieties offer superior disease resistance, important because healthy leaves mean more flowers. Verbenas are a host plant for swallowtail butterflies and a nectar favorite of bees.

Attractive alone in hanging baskets and pedestal pots, verbenas also shine in combination with other perennials and annuals. In pots and garden beds, they supply the "filler" element essential to harmonious designs. Combined with spiky plants or ones with round flowers, leafy trailing verbena fills the space around and between the others with flower clusters near ground level.

Verbena loses its perennial life in heavy, wet, winter soils, but will thrive when planted in very well-drained soils. If soils are especially dense, plant verbena in containers. Water new transplants with root-stimulating fertilizer. Keep watered well until established, then as conditions require. Verbenas are people-friendly plants; if you fertilize every other week and clip off old flowers and scraggly stems regularly, this plant will respond with bountiful blooms for months.

Shop locally for verbenas; some carry the same name in different places. 'Homestead Purple' is a classic, but so vigorous as to take over most landscapes. 'Biloxi Blue' and verbenas in the 'Twilight' series are newer, tidier choices. The fragrant 'Port Gibson Pink' offers distinctive cottage style; its blossoms bear several pink shades on each flower.

Potential problems: spider mites will attack dry plants; water underneath the leaves regularly.

INDIAN PINK
Spigelia marilandica
Category: partial-shade native perennial
Use: massed in beds for late spring, early summer flowers
Soil: well-drained, organic
Hardiness: zones 6–9
Mature size: 18" to 24" tall

Sometimes a plant's name can be confusing, and Indian pink is a good example. It is native to the Southeast, but not pink at all. Perhaps it should be called 'American red' or 'Starflower' for the yellow stars that emerge from red tubular flowers each spring. Or 'Neatnik' for its tidy clump and mirror-perfect pairs of leaves. Indian pink is an essential perennial for shady garden beds, and is among the best native plants introduced to southern landscapes in recent years.

ABOVE: Verbena (*Verbena canadensis*)
BELOW: Indian pink (*Spigelia marilandica*)

Salvia (*Salvia guaranitica*)

Combined with hardy ferns, Indian pink invokes a natural, woodland style in the garden. For an especially elegant combination, put the large, light green fronds of southern shield fern behind Indian pinks, and put carpet bugleweed in front. Plant Indian pink clumps with hostas alongside and elephant ear and bananas behind for an instant tropical atmosphere.

Grow Indian pink in soil enriched with organic matter, and space young plants 12" apart. Dig a hole wider and slightly deeper than the plant's rootball, backfill with amended soil, and plant it at the same depth it was growing in the container.

Soak Indian pink clumps deeply once a week during dry weather, especially in late winter. Keep 1" to 2" of organic mulch around the plant all year long. Fertilize in spring with a granular, slow-release formula, then work in 1" of compost around each plant annually after it flowers. Watch for seeds to mature in summer and collect them to plant in spring. Take root cuttings and divide the crowded plants in autumn. Replant these divisions or pot them up; bury root cuttings shallowly in a mix of potting soil and sand.

Potential problems: no pests are reported in healthy stands of Indian pink.

ARGENTINE SAGE
Salvia guaranitica
Category: sun-loving perennial
Use: in summer beds for the bold texture of blue flowers
Soil: fertile, very well-drained
Hardiness: zones 7–9
Mature size: 28" to 36"

If you like ruby-throated hummingbirds, Argentine salvia belongs in your garden. Leafy, dense, and coarse-textured, it can grow huge, commonly reaching 3' to 5' each summer. The larger this salvia gets, the more spiky blue flowers there are, soaring to attract the rubies. Also a fine cut flower, its long spikes add an airy touch to the vase as well as the perennial border.

The flowers are light blue in 'Argentine Sky' and true blue in 'Costa Rica'. Other shades of dark blue and purple are also available and as reliably dramatic. As the tallest plant in any combination of sun-loving perennials, this salvia grows into a big, round, shrub-like plant. Its medium-green color and texture make a nice contrasting backdrop for verbena, coleus, and zinnias.

Like many perennials, Argentine salvia's success ultimately depends on the survival of its crown. Excellent drainage in organic, fertile soil will sustain it for years. Amend heavy soils to improve drainage; plant in raised beds or on elevated island beds. Space plants 36" apart, or if planting only one, place other plants 18" away from it. It will fill the space rapidly.

Plants that grow this large each year are often heavy feeders, including Argentine salvia. Begin by using a granular flower formula fertilizer when new growth emerges, and again in the month of May. Water weekly to soak; add a soluble fertilizer every three weeks. Keep old flowers clipped off to encourage new ones, and cut stressed plants back by half at midsummer.

Potential problems: cold, wet soils can rot the crown; cut stems back after frost and mulch around the crown for winter protection.

ROSE MALLOW
Hibiscus moscheutos
Category: sun or light-shade perennial
Use: in mixed perennial and annual beds for dramatic midsummer flowers
Soil: fertile, well-drained
Hardiness: zones 6–9
Mature size: 18" to 36", depending on variety

With names like 'Flare' and 'Disco Belle', you'd expect these varieties of rose mallow to be showy in the garden, and they are outstanding. But 'Frisbee' actually describes them best. Big, flat, and wide-faced, the flowers look like paper dinner plates on stems. The large petals resemble gently wrinkled crepe paper, in bold reds, stark whites with red centers, and irregularly splashed pinks. Rose mallow's tropical style starts in clumps of large, soft-looking, matte-green leaves ranging from 2' to 3' long. Those "smiley-face" flowers make excellent companions to verbena, lantana, and ornamental grasses, as well as to traditional tropical plants in the summer garden.

Prepare a garden bed for rose mallow by amending native soil with organic matter, if needed, to improve drainage. Place small plants 8" to 12" apart, depending on the expected mature size. Water in well immediately after planting and mulch around the base of each plant.

To keep rose mallow blooming, water it often and deadhead it; that is, cut off spent flowers to stimulate new buds through the summer until frost bites the plant. Once it is all brown, cut back the top growth and refresh the mulch around the crown to protect it. Fertilize in March, May, and July with a granular flower formula, preferably one with some slow-release elements. Water well weekly during the growing season, more often if plants wilt in the afternoon.

Look for 'Moy Grande', the largest rose mallow of its kind, developed in Texas and named for its breeder. 'Moy' boasts rose-red, 12"-wide blossoms on a very tall, upright vase-shaped plant.

Potential problems: skeletonizing insects may devour all but the framework of leaves; remove damaged leaves and dust or spray with pyrethrin at the first sign of this pest.

COUNTRY GIRL CHRYSANTHEMUM
Chrysanthemum (Dendranthema zawadskii) 'Clara Curtis'
Category: sun, partial-shade perennial
Use: for pink daisies in fall
Soil: well-drained, fertile, organic
Hardiness: zones 6–9
Mature size: 18" to 24"

Tall and deep green, 'Clara Curtis' grows steadily all summer until finally dozens of perfectly round pink daisies pop open. At that point, the Country Girl, as it is also known, often flops over and blooms right on through the fall. Reliable, perennial, and seemingly immune to heat and humidity, this flamboyant flower may be the only mum to grow in the southern garden for the long haul.

No mum is as easy to grow as Country Girl. Sunny garden beds full of perennial salvia, rose mallow, and this mum can deliver flowers until the first killing frost. Choose a shorter perennial

ABOVE: Rose mallow (*Hibiscus moscheutos*)
BELOW: Country Girl mum (*Chrysanthemum* 'Clara Curtis')

or annual to grow in front of 'Clara Curtis' to give the flowers a place to land if they flop over, and to mask the lower, often leafless stems. For example, *Sedum* 'Lamb's Ears' and fernleaf yarrow offer bold contrast in leaves sturdy enough to catch the 'Clara Curtis' when it falls.

Small plants are available in early spring, and because 'Clara Curtis' reproduces so readily in the garden, plants are often offered at plant swaps and benefit sales. Amend the soil to enrich it organically and improve its drainage. Space 4"-tall plants 6" apart in the bed. Mulch to prevent weeds.

Water regularly to prevent drought that can delay or stop flowering. Pinch the tops out of the plants monthly from April through June to encourage bushy growth. However, 'Clara Curtis' will often outgrow its space and reproduce wildly. Dig up clumps and divide them every other year.

Potential problems: few pests on healthy plants.

BULBS

DAFFODIL
Narcissus 'Ice Capades'
Category: sun or shade bulb
Use: for late winter flowers
Soil: well-drained, fertile
Hardiness: zones 6–9
Mature size: 8" to 14"

Just when it seems the garden has lost all color except gray and brown, when even the nandinas have lost their red berries, the daffodils begin to bloom. The world is renewed, right there in the backyard, by the introduction of daffodils to every garden bed. Reliable and long-lived, your children can plant these daffodils and cut flowers every year until eventually they dig up some of the bulbs for their first garden. Select sunny or partly shady beds for daffodils under deciduous trees, along paths, and in large containers with panolas and pansies. Daffodils are excellent bedmates to long-lived perennials and roses. 'Ice Capades' is unbeatable for its garden performance, sporting large flowers with pale cream halos around yellow cups that age to nearly white.

Daffodils will be in the ground for many years, and often have plants on top of them. Great drainage is their biggest demand and is readily achieved by the addition of organic matter to the native soil. Select the largest bulbs available for the variety, and plant at a depth no more than twice the height of the bulb. Space daffodils 4" to 8" apart, depending on mature plant size. Lay out all the bulbs before planting to avoid confusion as to their location. Fertilize at planting time with a granular bulb formula, then use a complete garden fertilizer each spring after the flowers finish.

Excellent varieties for naturalizing include 'Tête-à-Tête', 'Unsurpassable', 'Hawera', 'Carlton', 'Fortune', and the classic *Narcissus* 'Paperwhite'.

Potential problems: if bulbs bloom less during one season than the last, they have sunk or become crowded; dig, divide, and replant, or share with friends.

Daffodil (*Narcissus* 'Ice Capades')

ABOVE: Swamp spider lily (*Hymenocallis* spp.)
BELOW: Red spider lily (*Lycoris radiata*)

SWAMP SPIDER LILY
Hymenocallis spp.
Category: sun or partial-shade native bulb
Use: for tropical texture, stunning flowers in summer
Soil: organic, fertile, well-drained or not
Hardiness: zones 7–10
Mature size: 24" to 30"

Luckily for gardeners, some of the great native plants you see on a walk through the woods can easily be grown in home landscapes. Few are as memorable as the swamp spider lily, its crown of white flowers open wide like hands with the skinniest, most graceful fingers you'll ever see. The flowers look like they are floating above a sea of green swords, a stunning and decidedly tropical scene. Swamp spiders naturally go well with banana plants, canna lilies, and hardy ferns, because they are versatile. Though native to the swamps of the southeastern United States, this bulb adapts equally well to organic, fertile soils that drain well. Use it in bog gardens with Louisiana iris, alongside streams and water features with flag iris, or with other perennials and bulbs in traditional borders that are watered regularly. Pure white, its flowers go with anything, and its effect on the mood in the garden is cooling.

Plant swamp spider lilies where they can be seen at dusk or are lit after dark when their angelic white glow can be appreciated. Prepare the soil for swamp spider lilies by digging and amending it with organic matter to enrich and increase its fertility. Plant bulbs about 15" apart and just less than 1" below soil level. Each spring when the new growth starts, put granular fertilizer in a circle around each bulb. Repeat in May. Keep watered very well from spring until the flowers finish. Remove old leaves after they turn brown in the late fall.

In addition to several native swamp spider lilies, Peruvian daffodil (*H. narcissiflora*) grows hardily across the South.

Potential problems: to prevent leaf scorch in full-sun sites, water frequently.

RED SPIDER LILY
Lycoris radiata
Category: light shade bulb
Use: in beds and lawns for surprising fall flowers
Soil: moderately well-drained
Hardiness: zones 6–9
Mature size: 12" to 14"

Late summer tests many plants—and gardeners—with hot, humid days and nights, often dry for a week, followed by torrential rain. Overnight, or so it seems, red spider lilies pop up in lawns and garden beds, each flower a spiny whirligig of deep coral petals and stamens atop glassine green stems. The bulbs make themselves right at home, spread underground, and bloom happily each year just in time to break up the summer doldrums. After the flowers, a neat clump of strappy leaves marks their spot all winter, then disappears as weather heats up in spring. They're gone, and then they're back, like the inevitable cool breezes of autumn.

Red spider lilies can grow almost anywhere you can dig a hole, but better-drained soils encourage their height and spread. Their adaptability makes them ideal for difficult spaces, or as a companion to cast-iron plant (*Aspidistra*) and ground covers in beds around big trees. Line a path, add interest to a hedge, dot the fenceline with them, or fill the space between close-set houses. Use red spider lilies as accents in the perennial border to bridge the gap between summer and fall bloomers. Fertilize red spider lilies annually when the leaves are present, and water weekly in dry summers to promote flowering.

Red spider lilies are the best known *Lycoris,* but 'Alba', a white variety, is also available. A close relative, known as naked ladies (*L. squamigera*), is larger, with big pink trumpets on leafless stems. Yellow spider lily (*L. aurea*) also does well in the deep South. None of these are as prolific as the red spider lilies, but are equally reliable bloomers.

Potential problems: no pests are reported on spider lilies.

GRASSES

DWARF SWEET FLAG
Acorus pramineus
Category: sun or partial-shade ornamental grass
Use: for texture and color
Soil: organic, fertile, well-drained or not
Hardiness: zones 5–9
Mature size: 12" to 14"

Dwarf sweet flag is small, with leaves as colorful as the banner of any nation. It is a handy plant in beds and mixed pots, serving as the classic "filler" to complement round and spiky shapes. Plant a clump or two by the water feature, more at the corner of a sunny bed; add a spray falling out of a pot full of snapdragons and petunias, or even a bit under the clematis vine as living mulch. Strappy green leaves with cream or gold variegation simply glow in sun, part shade, and night lighting.

Dwarf sweet flag appreciates an organic, fertile soil, wet or dry. Prepare the soil for this long-lived perennial before purchasing plants in spring. Position the clumps so their natural drape falls in the direction you want it to go. Dwarf sweet flag will thicken but generally won't change its natural path.

Mulch to repress weeds and keep rootzone shaded and moist between waterings. If growing in garden beds or pots, fertilize in early spring and again in June with a slow-release, nitrogen-rich granular garden formula. Where its roots grow into the water (as on the pond bank), dwarf sweet flag will usually get all the fertilizer it needs from that used in the pond for lilies and other aquatic plants. Cut back any leaves that become damaged or unattractive any time during the season.

Dwarf sweet flag (*Acorus gramineus*)

ABOVE: Muhly grass (*Muhlenbergia capillaris*)
BELOW: Maiden grass (*Miscanthus sinensis*)

'Variegatus' dwarf sweet flag is most popular, with streaks the color of fresh cream. 'Licorice' smells like its name when touched; plant it where passersby will brush it frequently.

Potential problems: no significant pests bother dwarf sweet flag.

MUHLY GRASS
Muhlenbergia capillaris
Category: sun-loving native ornamental grass
Use: for fine texture and lavender flowers in fall
Soil: well-drained, fertile
Hardiness: zones 6–9
Mature size: 24" to 36"

Muhly grass in bloom on a late summer day looks like a daydream feels, its incredible flowers an almost opaque deep pink cloud full of everything your heart desires. Clumps of thinly cut, fine-textured leaves grow into a rather spiky mound, just stiff enough to make pleasant rustling sounds in the lightest wind. Surprising, because it is a recent addition to the garden palette, muhly grass is a native of the Southeast. Its popularity spread by word of mouth because its beauty is unparalleled in the summer and fall garden. Planted in a large bed with joe-pye weed and 'Clara Curtis' mums, its effect is cooling and breezy, all cotton candy pink on a hot autumn afternoon.

Muhly grass needs a fertile, very well-drained soil to sustain its clump from year to year. Dig a wide hole and space plants 2' apart. Plant at the same height it was growing in the container, or a bit higher, as on a mound or at the raised center of an island bed. Water in well, but do not rush to water as the plants are getting established. After that, water regularly during the summer to promote flowering, but back off in winter and early spring.

Overwatering, especially in cold soils, can rot the clump. Fertilize muhly grass each year with a granular complete fertilizer in early spring and again in summer. After three seasons, dig, divide, and replant, or pot up to share with friends in the early spring. Mulch to prevent weeds with 1" of ground bark or pinestraw.

Potential problems: few pests are reported.

MAIDEN GRASS
Miscanthus sinensis
Category: sun-loving ornamental
Use: to span seasons in beds and borders
Soil: well-drained
Hardiness: zones 6–9
Mature size: 3' to 5' in bloom

Maiden grass retains its basic round mounded shape in southern gardens for ten months out of the year and creates the perfect backdrop for any sunny bed. Perhaps its best season is winter, when all else in the perennial border has gone dormant.

Also called silver grass and sometimes eulalia grass, maiden grass spans the region. At home in the coldest areas, it is undaunted by heat and high humidity. Clumps average 4' tall with equal diameter, with slender green leaves and warm, cream-colored, fringy flowers. Other family members offer silver-green, gray, and gold-striped leaves and flower plumes in pink, white, or silver.

A location with a little shade or one in full sun is preferred for maiden grass. As it is a large plant, give it room and a deep rootzone. Dig native soil to a depth of at least 8", amend for good drainage and fertility, then till well and rake into a low mound. Space maiden grass at least 4' apart and plant at the same depth it was growing in the container or slightly higher in shallow or very dense soils. Mulch lightly.

Keep maiden grasses watered during the summer to sustain their flowers, but do not overwater, especially right after winter pruning. Cut the grass clump down to ground level each January; fertilize then and again at midsummer with a slow-release formula. Dig up the clump and divide it every three years, even if it takes an axe to cut it apart. Overgrown, aging clumps will shatter, losing their form and creating a sprawling mess in the garden.

Potential problems: few pests are reported.

ANNUALS

SPIDER FLOWER
Cleome hassleriana
Category: sun or light shade annual
Use: in groups for flowers and height in summer
Soil: well-drained, fertile, organic
Hardiness: zones 6–9
Mature size: 24" to 40" depending on variety

Spider flower will spice up any garden bed with delightfully bizarre flowers bursting from tall stems lined with stiff, smelly, sticky leaves, especially in the grand old 'Queen' cleomes. Their flowerheads, each with scores of petals that shoot out dozens of skinny sepals, nod in the least breeze. Their weight leads to a graceful, slightly arched profile, an excellent choice for the center of an island bed in the lawn.

Perhaps because of its distinctive aroma and furry foliage, spider flower used to be a "love it or hate it" plant. But the slightly less aromatic 'Sparkler', noted for its neater habit, shorter stems, and plants that branch at ground level, introduced this delightfully southern plant to many more gardens. Both types deliver hummingbird-loving, airy carousels of flowers in white, pink, and purple shades. Spider flowers are dramatic against a backdrop of ornamental grasses or alone in front of a dog-eared fence. They are not difficult to grow, but will be stunted by prolonged droughts, so they are perfect candidates for planting along a soaker hose.

Spider flower (*Cleome hassleriana*)

Impatiens (*Impatiens walleriana*)

Plant spider flowers in soil amended as needed to enrich it and improve its drainage. Dig the hole a bit larger than the rootball, and if the roots are tightly wound, tear them slightly before planting. Watering deeply once a week or more often in hot, dry weather will sustain plants and flowers; use fertilizer through the season if needed.

Potential problems: no pests; if they reseed to excess, remove seedpods before they open and keep the plants mulched.

IMPATIENS
Impatiens walleriana
Category: shade annual
Use: in containers or massed in beds for spring, summer, and fall color
Soil: well-drained, organic, fertile
Hardiness: all zones
Mature size: 8" to 20", depending on selection

Shade-loving impatiens are everywhere, ringing trees with color, lining shady paths, and spilling from containers. Each year brings a new twist on these time-honored annuals; each new one is pure "eye candy" for gardeners. Smaller selections, variegated leaves, double flowers, and new color combinations offer a series of impatiens for every shade garden. 'Super Elfin' (less than 12" tall) can edge the border, whereas 'Tempo' (often 2' tall) stands behind an edge of monkey grass or lily turf. Distinctively different, double- or rose-flowered impatiens look like tiny roses, and mottled flowers in the 'Mosaic' series add depth and interesting hues. Truly tiny 'Pixie' impatiens can fill small pots in a shady gazebo or spill from an urn filled with caladium bulbs and ferns.

To prepare a garden bed for impatiens under a large tree, remember that it is not a good practice to add more than 1" of soil over tree roots. Step back and dig or till the bed a few feet away from the trunk to avoid its roots and to create a bed in visual proportion to the tree. Amend the soil to enrich and improve its drainage. Plant short impatiens on 6" centers, taller or spreading varieties 8" to 10" apart.

Water impatiens several times a week in hot weather, and fertilize at least once a month with a soluble formula. At any time during the season, you can cut back impatiens if they become leggy.

Potential problems: snails and slugs may attack young plants; reduce mulch and use iron phosphate barrier products or diatomaceous earth to deter them.

COLEUS
Solenostemon scutellarioides
Category: sun or shade annual
Use: for colorful leaves from spring through fall
Soil: well-drained, fertile
Hardiness: zones 6–9
Mature size: 18" to 24"

Coleus comes and goes as a garden favorite, but it should be a staple everywhere. Easy to grow, coleus fills its space rapidly with pointed or round leaves bursting with color. Some have ruffled edges, other are bicolors with streaks and stripes, and some recall abstract paintings. New and improved varieties offer colors across the spectrum. Look for 'New Orleans Red' in bright burgundy, and 'Alabama Sunset' in shades of yellow and coral, any coleus named 'Solar', and the old favorite, 'Tilt-a-Whirl'.

Take advantage of this versatile plant for sun and shade with this caveat: the more green found in the leaf, the more shade the coleus can stand. Grow from small transplants purchased in early spring; single-pattern leaves and mixes are widely available. Space standard types 12" apart in well-drained soil, smaller types only slightly closer together. Plant coleus in groups among other annuals such as spider flower and zinnia, or fill a bed in a rainbow of reliable color all summer.

Plants with square stems, like coleus, mint, and lantana, have a common trait: they like to be pinched. That is, each time you pinch out the tip cluster of leaves, the plants respond with more growing points below the pinch. The result can be bushy coleus, nearly 3' tall and covered in wildly hued leaves. After coleus finishes flowering, it will be spent. Remove flower stalks as soon as they appear, and give them a pinch then, too. Water deeply once a week and add fertilizer twice each month.

Potential problems: if sticky white mealybugs appear, use insecticidal soap or pyrethrin.

PANOLA
Viola cornuta 'Panola'
Category: sun and partial-shade annual
Use: in beds and pots in fall, winter, and spring
Soil: very well-drained, fertile, organic
Hardiness: zones 6–9
Mature size: 9" to 12"

The sweet faces of pansies and the neater forms of violas combine in panolas. Even better for gardeners, they're proving to be easier to grow than either of their parents, the hallmark of a great hybrid plant. When planted in fall, the flowers of this family of plants glow like jewels against the duller grays and browns of the southern winter and continue well into spring. Easier to grow than fall garden mums and longer-blooming, they are the most dependable flowers to grow over winter in the South.

ABOVE: Coleus (*Solenostemon scutellarioides*)
BELOW: Panola (*Viola cornuta* 'Panola')

Available in a bright mix of colors and flower types, including solids, bicolors, and blends, with characteristic faces, panolas are undeniably cheery in containers and as ground cover below spring-flowering bulbs. Perhaps their best quality is resilience; after winter storms they come back strong.

Well-drained, fertile, and organic soil will sustain the pansy family for many months in the garden or container. Amend 4" of native soil with an equal amount of organic matter and till together, then rake smooth. Space plants 4" to 6" apart, water in well, and apply 2" of organic mulch.

Panolas, improved johnny jump-ups like the 'Sorbet' series, and improved pansies 'Majestic Giant' and 'Bingo' are easy to grow. Water pansies frequently until the plants are well established, then as often as needed to prevent wilting. Use granular garden fertilizer regularly or a soluble formula once a month to keep new leaves and flowers coming.

Potential problems: few pests pose major problems to panolas and their relatives.

SNAPDRAGON
Antirrhinum majus
Category: sun and light-shade annual
Use: for beds, mostly spring bloom but some fall
Soil: very well-drained, organic, fertile
Hardiness: zones 6–9
Mature size: 16" to 24"

Snapdragons are unsurpassed for elegance in the garden and the vase. Stiffly erect, their stems are dense, with soft-looking green leaves. The honeycomb of leaves gives way to flower clusters, pyramids of color that open from bottom to top over a few days. Short, medium, and tall height varieties, along with trailing snapdragons, offer a host of design possibilities in beds and containers. Spiky snapdragons are a perfect complement to spring-flowering bulbs like daffodils, tulips, and Dutch iris. Plants appear in the garden centers in fall along with panolas, pansies, and ornamental cabbages. A cluster of snapdragons adds its upright multitude of tiny flowers to their big round faces and shapes to good effect; both are more attractive when contrasted with each other.

Dozens of snapdragons are available in a rainbow of colors; shop locally for hometown favorite varieties. In general, the trailing and dwarf varieties bloom first, followed by taller ones, and finally the stately, 6" to 32" varieties like the 'Liberty Classic' series.

Cold, wet soils can stunt snapdragons, or worse. Prepare a well-drained, organic, and fertile soil for these long-lived annuals and their companions. Plant bulbs first if possible, or mark space for them, then put snapdragons in place for clumps or lines of color. Water in well after planting and mulch well. Water often until the plants are established and the weather cools. Fertilize at least monthly during the growing season, but more often if weather is very mild. Keep garden plants deadheaded, but cut flowers for the vase once half the cluster is open.

Potential problems: few pests are troublesome to snapdragons, but icy winters can be.

Snapdragon (*Antirrhinum majus*)

ABOVE: 'Wave' petunia (*Petunia* x *hybrida* 'The Wave')
BELOW: Madagascar periwinkle (*Catharanthus roseus*)

'WAVE' PETUNIAS
Petunia x *hybrida* 'The Wave'
Category: sun annual
Use: in beds and containers for long-blooming color
Soil: very well-drained, fertile
Hardiness: zones 6–8 (annual); zone 9 (perennial)
Mature size: 14" to 18" (others vary)

Petunias used to be just a springtime annual, but the 'Waves' changed all that in the 1990s. Beautiful, reliable, and available in more colors and sizes each year, these petunias can bloom nearly nonstop for all but the coldest months of the year. Some even perennialize in hospitable microclimates in zones 8 and 9. First came 'Purple Wave', a blanket of trumpets on a flat bed of green; soon its closest relatives, other ground cover 'Waves', found their way to beds and huge hanging baskets. 'Easy Waves' and 'Tidal Waves' offer equally long-blooming flowers on larger plants that spread, trail, and mound. Some suit beds by themselves, others crawl along in front of daylilies and irises, and still others are perfect for annual beds with coleus and spider flower.

Provide well-drained, fertile soil for 'Wave' petunias. Purchase small transplants in spring, and space as directed on the label. Or plant large containers for instant color, allowing 2" of space between the leaves of one plant and another. Water in well and mulch lightly.

'Wave' petunias are called heavy feeders, indicating their need for regular fertilizing. Use granular garden fertilizer monthly or soluble flower formula every two weeks. Cut back plants if they become leggy to encourage new growth.

Others to consider are the old-fashioned, reseeding, fragrant petunias. Not the easiest to seed, but well worth the effort. Also look for the 'Madness' series for excellent thunderstorm recovery in rainy areas.

Potential problems: slugs and snails can devour new transplants; use diatomaceous earth or iron phosphate baits as a barrier around each plant and keep mulch to a minimum.

MADAGASCAR PERIWINKLE
Catharanthus roseus 'Pacifica'
Category: sun annual
Use: fill beds and containers for flowers all summer
Soil: very well-drained, fertile
Hardiness: all zones
Mature size: 12" to 20"

This delightful periwinkle might be called the "procrastinator's plant." If you're busy all spring and keep putting off going to the garden center for annuals to color up those beds and containers, plant Madagascar periwinkle in latest spring and it will bloom from summer until frost. Flowers shaped like windmill blades bloom atop glossy, rounded, oval-shaped leaves. Each stem bears a cluster of five-petaled flowers, many with contrasting centers. Madagascar periwinkle is a high-impact plant in the landscape, loved for neat form, easy care, and spectacular flowers in a range of colors from white through salmon and coral to red and lavender blues.

Periwinkles named 'Pacifica' set the bar high for compact plants with plenty of flowers that are known as self-cleaning. That means they fall neatly to the ground and disappear, maintaining their neat looks without much deadheading. Periwinkles named 'Cooler', 'Sunstorm', and 'Heatwave' are also reliable and readily available.

Planting periwinkles in cold soil is fruitless. At best, they sit there and never grow; at worst, they die. Prepare the soil as for other annuals to improve drainage, adding organic matter to enrich it, and plant earlier-blooming annuals like zinnias and spider flowers in the bed. But leave room for periwinkles across the front of the bed for nonstop summer flowering from all three. In the right place at the right time, periwinkle care is simple. Water slowly to soak the bed once a week, if rain is not ample.

Potential problems: few pests are reported, but overwatering and very rainy weather can cause the plants to become stunted.

ZINNIA
Zinnia elegans x *hybrida* 'Profusion'
Category: sun-loving annual
Use: in beds for summer flowers
Soil: well-drained, fertile
Hardiness: all zones
Mature size: 16" for 'Profusion'; others vary

Zinnias are a garden staple with spunky stems, fuzzy matte-green leaves, and flowers shaped like saucers, stars, and pom-poms in every color but true blue. Their effect is cheery and they are long-lived in bed and vase. All three 'Profusion' zinnias (white, orange, and cherry) were awarded the All America Selections Gold Medal for superior garden performance. Their disease resistance, drought tolerance, and long blooming season make 'Profusion' a winner for southern gardens; they require only minimal attention. Their name comes from the huge number of flowers each plant yields from spring through the end of autumn.

Good drainage and fertile soil are the keys to great zinnias of all sorts. Space zinnias to allow good air circulation around mature plants; for 'Profusion' zinnias, 12" apart. Larger standard zinnias like 'Dreamland' should be spaced 18" apart; little ones 8" apart such as the pom-pom—flowered 'Peter Pan'. Water well after planting, then only as often as necessary to prevent wilting. Fertilize every other week with a soluble flower formula.

The more zinnias you cut for bouquets, the more buds a healthy plant will make. If plants lose their good looks at midsummer, cut back and continue watering and fertilizing for autumn flowers. This works especially well on 'Profusion'; many consider it the best zinnia for the fall garden.

Narrow leaf zinnias (*Z. angustifolia*) like 'Crystal White' have also won awards for their beauty and durability; space them 12" apart in order to grow into spheres covered with small flowers.

Potential problems: treat leaf spots with dusting sulfur or flower garden dust.

Zinnia (*Zinnia elegans* x *hybrida*)

ABOVE: Moonflower (*Ipomoea alba*)
BELOW: Coral honeysuckle (*Lonicera sempervirens*)

VINES

🌿

MOONFLOWER
Ipomoea alba 'Giant White'
Category: sun annual
Use: in summer for fragrant flowers and shade
Soil: organic, fertile
Hardiness: zones 6–8 (annual); zone 9 (perennial)
Mature size: 30'

Plants such as magnificent moonflower that bloom at night add instant romance to the garden. The sight and scent of an arbor bursting with scores of the sweet-smelling, creamy-white trumpets in full bloom are unforgettable. Because its only daylight attraction is 30' of vigorous green vine, moonflower is often planted with its relative, morning glory, for twenty-four hours of flowers, summer until frost. Add four o'clocks in front of the two vines to mark time in a classic clock garden.

Fast-growing moonflower vine delivers the goods to gardeners impatient for shade, eager for flower blankets, and challenged by small spaces. Grow them to decorate a courtyard wall, create a better view, or cool off the patio. All it takes is a strong support trellis and a packet of seeds. The planting space for moonflowers can be narrow, so long as the soil is organic and fertile. Moonflower seed coats are hard, so help by breaking them to encourage faster sprouting; scratch their surface with an emery board or cut a nick in them, then soak overnight before planting. Gently push each seed 1" deep into the soil and cover it. Water in well and look for sprouts in seven to ten days. Keep the area weeded and start the vines up their trellis by hand; they'll take over from there. Water to soak the rootzone weekly or more often in very hot weather. Fertilize monthly if needed to encourage vines.

For even more romance, grow another moonflower relative, Spanish flag (*I. lobata*).

Potential problems: water the backs of the vines occasionally to deter spider mites.

CORAL HONEYSUCKLE
Lonicera sempervirens
Category: sun or part shade native perennial
Use: trumpet-shaped flowers on dense, woody vine
Soil: well-drained, fertile
Hardiness: zones 4–9
Mature size: 20'

To cover an arbor, create a screen, and attract hummingbirds with one plant, choose coral honeysuckle, the easiest to grow of all the trumpet honeysuckles. This perennial vine will lose its leaves in zone 7 and upper 8, then return in spring with soft blue-green new leaves 2" to

3" long. Elsewhere, it is nearly evergreen and in bloom as much as eight months of the year. Its red coral trumpets turn their bells slightly upward, holding their nectar out for hungry mouths.

A neat grower, native coral honeysuckle never invades like its relative, Japanese honeysuckle. It will not take over shrubs, but is simple to propagate from tip or root cuttings. 'Coral honeysuckle' is usually the name on tags identifying this wonderful native vine, but selections from it are equally beautiful if not quite as vigorous. 'Sulphurea' has yellow flowers; 'Alabama Scarlet' bears its namesake color. Some areas favor scarlet trumpet honeysuckle (*L.* x *brownii* 'Dropmore Scarlet').

Full-sun sites bring out the best in this vine, but lightly shaded locations work as well. This honeysuckle's nemesis is tightly packed clay soil, so amend as needed to provide very good drainage. Dig a hole deeper and wider than the rootball, then put enough soil back into the hole to install the plant at the same depth it was growing in the pot. Water in well, and keep watered until established.

Keep mulch around the base of the vine and fertilize in spring with a granular formula. Prune between flowerings and water more often when in bloom.

Potential problems: few pests are reported on healthy vines.

CLEMATIS
Clematis x *lanuginosa* 'Nelly Moser'
Category: sun or light-shade perennial
Use: for abundant spring flowers on neat woody vine
Soil: fertile, organic, very well-drained
Hardiness: zones 4–9
Mature size: 15' on average

Clematis dazzles with star-shaped, richly colored flowers with long, often striped petals surrounding a spiky yellow bright center. Because it is fast growing but not huge, the clematis vine is remarkably hardy and simple to maintain in garden beds and borders.

'Nelly Moser' is a southern favorite clematis, with pink flower petals striped with lavender rose that last for days. Each local area offers selections noted for their durability, but for huge white flowers, 'Henryii' is unsurpassed, and for purple-blue flowers, 'Star of India' may be the best known.

Very well-drained soil that never heats up provides the best environment for clematis. Amend the soil as needed, or grow the vine in a slightly raised bed. Dig a hole deeper and slightly wider than the rootball, and handle with care as these roots can be slow to repair after transplant. Add 2" of mulch to the base of the vine, or plant a discreet perennial to shade and cool the roots, such as dwarf sweet flag.

Fertilize in spring and summer with a granular garden fertilizer, and replenish mulch often. Cut the vine back as needed within one month after bloom. Often this job is neglected for several years; it should not be.

Summer- and fall-blooming clematis are not as widely grown, but should be given more consideration. Fragrant and a bit rampant, autumn clematis deserves a place in the woodland

Clematis (*Clematis* x *lanuginosa*)

Fringe flower (*Loropetalum Chinense*)

garden, where it can climb freely. Cut back these later-season clematis vines in early spring.

Potential problems: few pests are reported on healthy vines.

SHRUBS

REDLEAF FRINGE FLOWER
Loropetalum chinense var. rubrum
Category: sun or light-shade evergreen
Use: as hedges or massed in beds for colorful leaves and flowers
Soil: organic, fertile, well-drained
Hardiness: zones 7–9
Mature size: 10' (selections vary from 4' to 15')

First exhibited in the United States in the 1990s, redleaf fringe flower created a firestorm of interest for its round, purplish red and green leaves studded with clusters of flower tubes in neon shades. Early varieties featured hot pink flowers and new growth that was either red-purple ('Burgundy') or bronze-purple ('Blush'). These popular evergreen shrubs are readily maintained as a 6'-tall hedge that blooms mostly in spring.

Smaller varieties of fringe flower have become a staple in street-side beds and foundation plantings where shrubs of 3' to 4' are preferred. Their names can be very confusing, with the same plant going by different monikers, depending on the region and grower. Shop while the plants are in bloom if you have a particular shade of pink in mind. Some retain all their purple leaf tones; others naturally green as they age. White-flowered fringe flower is also stunning, since its leaves are the darkest of all.

Consistently moist, very fertile organic soil that drains well contributes to strong leaf color in fringe flower. Plant at the depth it was growing in the container in a hole slightly deeper and wider than the rootball. Space large types 6' apart, smaller ones 3' apart. Water in well and add 2" of organic mulch to the soil surface. Use a granular fertilizer with a formula made for acid-loving plants (such as azaleas) in the spring and again in summer. Keep watered regularly and replenish mulch as needed.

Potential problems: leaves can yellow between their veins; add iron and increase organic matter.

DWARF HOLLY
Ilex cornuta 'Carissa'
Category: sun or part shade evergreen
Use: as low hedge or foundation planting
Soil: fertile, well-drained
Hardiness: zones 6–9
Mature size: 3' to 6' tall and 4' to 6' wide

Slightly wider than they are tall, dwarf hollies are garden workhorses. Very easy to grow, they tolerate drought and full sun, but will do as well in light shade. With dark evergreen color year round, the dwarf hollies have excellent staying power, never wilting or losing their sheen. They respond well to annual pruning to keep their main stems actively growing, producing thick stands of sharply pointed leaves.

'Carissa' holly is not known for traditional berries, but for the elegantly thin, yellow edge that defines each leaf and sets it apart from other dwarf evergreen shrubs, including its relatives. For such a durable, reliable shrub, it looks remarkably sophisticated in the garden. That makes it eminently suitable for every garden style, from formal to cottage and everything in between.

Plant dwarf hollies 4' to 5' apart in soil that drains well and has been amended to ensure ample nutrients will be available. Water deeply but not frequently, and fertilize twice a year in spring and summer. Keep mulch to a minimum, and prune in late winter to keep the holly shrubs neatly shaped.

Dwarf 'Burford' holly is a favorite for its solid green leaves that curl under slightly and produce copious red berries, but is best used as a hedge as it will easily reach 6' tall or more. The native deciduous holly, or 'Possum Haw', is a distinctive tree (often a thicket), noted for its red berries that linger long after the leaves are gone. It is a favorite late-winter food source for birds.

Potential problems: few serious pests trouble healthy hollies. Control scale insects with horticultural oil.

AZALEA 'CORAL BELLS'
Rhododendron 'Coral Bells'
Category: part-shade semi-evergreen
Use: for foundation plantings or massed in beds for mostly spring flowers
Soil: organic, fertile, well-drained
Hardiness: zones 7–9
Mature size: 4' tall and slightly wider

From the big mounds and huge trumpets of Formosas to the little-leafed Kurumes to the beloved 'Coral Bells', flowers from white to red and every shade in between can literally cover the leaves in spring. These shrubs, large and small, often offer a decent splash of fall leaf color as they go dormant. And 'Encore' azaleas actually offer reliable fall-blooming selections with excellent garden performance in zones 7 through 9.

Azaleas are shallow-rooted but send out a wide network near the soil surface. Be sure the

ABOVE: Dwarf holly (*Ilex cornuta*)
BELOW: Azalea (*Rhododendron* 'Coral Bells')

American beautyberry (*Callicarpa americana*)

soil is well amended with organic matter to improve its drainage and to acidify it. Dig a hole twice as wide and a bit deeper than the rootball, then plant the azaleas "high." That means refill the hole with amended soil, nestle the azalea into the very top, then pull soil and mulch up around the base of the plant. Space plants according to their mature size to provide good air circulation around each plant. Water in well and blanket the soil surface with 2" of organic mulch.

With a simple annual care regime, azaleas can shine for years in light shade. Fertilize with an azalea formula when new growth begins in spring and again in late June. Water weekly in dry spells and prune to shape within one month of flowering.

Look for deciduous native azaleas for honeysuckle-like flowers on upright shrubs that will bloom in deeper shade than their modern counterparts. Amazing shades of yellow and orange as well as pink and white grace the native honeysuckles.

Potential problems: if insects are a continuing problem, switch to fertilizer containing systemic insecticide.

AMERICAN BEAUTYBERRY
Callicarpa americana
Category: sun or shade native deciduous
Use: for strong arching form, coarse texture, and purple berries
Soil: fertile, well-drained
Hardiness: zones 6–9
Mature size: 4' to 6' tall and wider

native beautyberry, outstanding in the woodland garden, is equally at home in mixed shrub beds with azaleas or fringe flower. Summer flowers are small and cannot rival the vivid purple berries for drama. Polished to a sheen and prized by birds, the seeds that do make it to ground often sprout, creating a natural thicket habitat. In sunny sites, the stems are thick with leaves; in shade, the growth is taller and sparser, but the berries are as plentiful. The best known of this plant group, American beautyberry reveals its native roots in coarse, rough-looking leaves 6" long that turn bright yellow before they fall.

Think of the floor of the woods when preparing to plant beautyberry. Prepare an organic, well-drained soil in an area large enough to let the plants spread as they age. Space the plants 2' apart, water in well, and mulch deeply with leaf mold. Keep the shrubs moist until well established.

If you make compost, or have a pile of leaves rotting behind the shed, replenish the 2" layer under the beautyberry regularly to fertilize it and suppress weeds. Otherwise, apply garden fertilizer in spring. Water regularly during dry seasons; do not let the plants wilt.

Japanese beautyberry is a fine choice for small space gardens, 3' to 4' tall and 5' wide and has small, lime-green leaves and small magenta berries.

Potential problems: if stems freeze to the ground, don't despair; new ones will replace them.

GARDEN ROSE
Rosa Knock Out™ or *R.* 'fuchsia meidiland'
Category: deciduous shrub
Use: for flowers and rounded shapes
Soil: organic, fertile, well-drained
Hardiness: zones 6–9
Mature size: 5' tall and as wide

If a garden could only have two flowers, chances are roses would be one. With so many colors and growth habits to choose from, roses could create a garden that would cover acres. Garden roses, prized for their landscape form and abundant, usually reblooming flowers, are as easy to grow as any other shrub and bloom for months in the South. Named appropriately, hardy, gorgeous Knock Out™ delivers dozens of truly red flowers in clusters and requires minimal care.

Long-lived in the garden, shrub roses thrive in full sun with well-drained soil. Dig a hole wider and slightly deeper than the rootball, and space the plants 18" to 24" apart or more, depending on mature size. Spacing for good air circulation around each plant is essential for healthy leaves and maximum growth. Fertilize in early spring and every other month until August if you want them to continue growing; if not, limit fertilizer to twice a season. Water regularly and keep 1" to 2" of organic mulch underneath.

Perhaps the best thing about garden roses is that they need to be pruned annually. That enables you to control their height and spread and keep new stems coming for more flowers. The second best thing may be that they can be pruned throughout the growing season to encourage more flowers and maintain their shape.

Reliable groups of true old garden roses include the Noisettes, Bourbons, and China roses. Newer, but very popular, especially in zones 7 and 8, are many of the David Austin roses. Meidiland roses deserve much more attention from gardeners, as does the 'Dream' series.

Potential problems: few pests bother garden roses.

LIGUSTRUM
Ligustrum japonicum 'Nobilis'
Category: sun or shade evergreen
Use: as hedges, foundation plantings, or border backdrops
Soil: fertile, well-drained
Hardiness: zones 7–10
Mature size: 8' to 12'

Southern garden stalwarts take everything our climate can dish out: heat, humidity, monsoons, drought, and less-than-wonderful soils. Like its frequent companion, heavenly bamboo, ligustrum is dependably beautiful as a hedge or background plant. Both evergreens define space year round and should be used to reinforce the garden's architecture. Ideal for hedges in every garden microclimate, older ligustrums can be pruned to remove their lower branches, creating outstanding small trees with attractive gnarly gray bark.

ABOVE: Shrub rose (*Rosa* Knock Out™)
BELOW: Ligustrum (*Ligustrum japonicum* 'Nobilis')

'Nobilis' outshines its relatives; its leaves, new and old, look freshly oiled every day. The late-spring flowers appear in large clusters, creamy cone shapes with a distinctive fragrance that is very attractive to bees. Clusters of dark purple berries have a delightful sheen to them and last until birds devour them in late winter.

Ligustrum comes in a variety of sizes and grows moderately fast. But for instant screens or border backdrops, select the largest your budget allows. Prepare a soil that drains well to encourage a deep root system and enhance drought tolerance. Dig a hole deeper and wider than the rootball, then refill it with amended soil and plant the ligustrum at the height it was growing in the container. Water in well and mulch with 2" of organic material.

Water deeply but not frequently, and fertilize ligustrum when new growth starts in spring and again in summer to grow the shrubs. After the shrubs reach the desired height and spread, fertilize once a year. Prune in late winter to shape and encourage new growth throughout the shrubs' branches. Additional pruning can be done in late spring to encourage more new growth and control height.

Potential problems: if blooms make you sneeze, cut off flowers before they open.

HEAVENLY BAMBOO
Nandina domestica 'Compacta'
Category: sun and shade evergreen
Use: as hedges, mixed shrub borders
Soil: well-drained, fertile
Hardiness: zones 6–9
Mature size: 3' to 4'

Heavenly bamboo has a delicate, airy look, but this shrub is no lightweight when it comes to enduring the whims of the southern climate. Gardens long ago abandoned still boast their canes and perky leaflets in every shade from green and yellow to purple and red. The little leaves arrange themselves into large triangular leaflets that jut out at right angles from very upright canes that do resemble bamboo. Heavenly bamboo's white flower clusters are waxy in spring, attractive to bees, and followed by bright red berries that truly shine in the winter garden and complement the season's camellias and lenten roses.

Heavenly bamboo is able to withstand anything except wet feet, so amend heavy soils to improve drainage. Space plants for their mature size, which ranges from 2' to 6'. Soak after transplanting, but do not overwater at any time. Keep mulched.

Fertilize in the spring with a granular formula; repeat in June in the first years after planting. As heavenly bamboos age, their canes may lose lower leaves and appear sparse. Cut them back to near ground level and fertilize to encourage new canes. Prune healthy nandinas only to remove damaged or overcrowded canes.

'Compacta' refines heavenly bamboo's best qualities with more and thinner canes on a 4' shrub with finer leaves, profuse berries, and some winter color. Other shrubs to consider are

Heavenly bamboo (*Nandina domestica* 'Compacta')

Oak (*Quercus*)

'Alba' (very light green leaves and cream-white berries) and 'Atropurpurea Nana' (no more than 2' tall, with very red leaves in winter). 'Umpqua Warrior' easily reaches 8' tall and makes an excellent tall barrier.

Potential problems: none.

TREES

OAK TREE
Quercus nuttallii or Q. shumardii
Category: sun-loving deciduous native
Use: for shades of red or yellow fall color
Soil: well-drained, fertile
Hardiness: zones 5–9
Mature size: 40' to 60"

Stately, long-lived oaks reach skyward with a sense of reassuring permanence. A mature oak provides shade under its canopy, wildlife food and habitat, fall color, and bushels of leaves for the compost heap. The leaves vary from small and spatula-shaped (water oak and live oak) to large and lobed (nuttall and shumard oak). Acorns range from the size of peas (red oak and Georgia oak) to the size of golf balls (overcup oak), decorated with jaunty caps above shiny, sometimes striped or spotted, nuts.

Both nuttall oak and its close relative, shumard oak, grow steadily if not quickly, display red bronze leaf color, and bear plentiful acorns—the largest difference between them is the nuttall's ability to tolerate wet soils. Their canopies soon lose their youthful pyramid shape and provide great shade.

Native oaks are not fussy about soil types, but will grow more steadily with improved drainage and fertility. Smaller trees are easier to transplant and less likely to need staking. Prepare the soil in an area three times as deep and twice as wide as the rootball, then refill the planting hole with amended soil as needed to plant the oak. Water in well and mulch around the tree to a depth of 2".

Keep trees watered in dry seasons and fertilize annually in spring and summer while the trees are young. Use a fall feeding formula in the early years if the trees are spindly. Mature trees benefit from annual applications of fertilizer to keep new growth healthy and prevent some diseases.

Potential problems: few pests bother oak trees.

ABOVE: Japanese maple (*Acer palmatum*)
BELOW: Crepe myrtle (*Lagerstroemia indica*)

JAPANESE MAPLE
Acer palmatum
Category: part shade or sun deciduous
Use: as focal point tree for its colorful leaves
Soil: well-drained, fertile
Hardiness: zones 6–9
Mature size: 20' (selections vary from 5' to 20')

Japanese maples' limbs stretch out wide at the base, growing shorter as they reach the top of a pyramid of branches, with delicately cut leaves that are pure green with red and gold tones at times. 'Red Japanese maples' display crimson to purple new growth that ages to green in summer, then turns red again in fall. Some selections, like 'Bloodgood', retain their deep red color all summer. There are tall Japanese maples, shorter mounded ones, and others that spill their branches into a weeping form with very fine cut leaves (called laceleafs).

Use Japanese maple as the focal point in a lightly shaded bed; sunny beds produce a dense maple, capable of shading bulbs and ground covers planted below it like carpet bugleweed. Excellent companion plants include daffodil, heavenly bamboo, dwarf holly, and dwarf sweet flag.

Well-drained soil allows maximum root growth and a large, healthy maple. Prepare the soil by amending with organic matter and fertilizer to improve its drainage and nutrition. Dig a hole wider and deeper than the rootball and plant the maple just higher than it was growing in the container. Pull soil and mulch up around its base and water in well. Continue to water frequently to prevent transplant stress.

Consistency is the key to caring for Japanese maples. The roots need very regular moisture to support the leaves, easily provided by soaker hoses or regular irrigation. Fertilize when new leaves appear in spring and repeat in summer while tree is young.

Potential problems: very wet conditions can cause leaf spot and early drop; discard all affected leaves and use fungicide on next new growth.

CREPE MYRTLE
Lagerstroemia 'Natchez' or *L. indica*
Category: sun or light shade deciduous
Use: as focal point tree for its summer flowers
Soil: well-drained, fertile, organic
Hardiness: zones 6–9
Mature size: 20'

Crepe myrtle blossoms, just before they open, are encased in shimmering, thin pods. It's a southern childhood tradition to pinch them open by squeezing the base, like a snapdragon or larkspur. But the crepe myrtle pops open like jack-in-the-box, with more ruffled petals than could possibly fit inside the pod. Each flowering stem on the crepe myrtle tree holds dozens of small pods that burst open in huge cones of color.

Sasanqua (*Camellia sasanqua*)

From classic, popular varieties like 'Watermelon Red' to weeping forms such as 'Near East', crepe myrtle has come a long way. 'Natchez' is among the best of the hybrids, boasting excellent disease resistance, peeling bark, and trademark flowers. Tall and spreading, the canopy often reaches 20', so it is best used as a focal-point tree, well away from any structure. Red-brown bark may peel with age; flowers are pure white.

Crepe myrtle will thrive in well-drained, organic soil that is moderately fertile. Prepare the soil for this long-lived tree to a depth and width at least twice that of its container. Space large growers 10' apart; smaller ones can be slightly closer, but leave room for their mature canopy to spread. Water the tree in well, soaking slowly to wet the entire rootzone. Mulch with 2" of organic material. Fertilize annually in spring and summer.

Crepe myrtle can be pruned while dormant in winter to shape the tree if needed. During the growing season, clip off old flowers to stimulate new ones.

Potential problems: piercing and sucking insects can dehydrate trees; use pyrethrins or oil spray.

SASANQUA
Camellia sasanqua
Category: shade evergreen
Use: in beds or borders for fall flowers
Soil: organic, fertile, well-drained
Hardiness: zones 7–9
Mature size: selections range from 2' to 15'

When fall perennials begin to fade, sasanquas light up the darkening days with bright red, white, and pink flowers that bloom for months. Single sasanqua flowers are 2" to 3" across and open-faced, with slightly ruffled, silky petals around a cluster of bright yellow stamens. Double-flowered sasanqua looks more like the famous blooms of relative, the camellia, but is decidedly more low-maintenance and less formal in appearance. Sasanqua reaches upward, its limbs in an open vase shape, while camellia is naturally more rounded.

Scores of sasanqua varieties crowd the garden centers in autumn. Classics include 'Mine-No-Yuki' or white doves (fine-textured leaves, white flowers), 'Cleopatra' (pinky-rose semidouble flowers noted for cold tolerance), and 'Yuletide' (red flowers on very upright plant).

Sasanqua can be grown in sun, but best maintains its glossy evergreen leaves with some afternoon shade. A site with light shade all day is ideal, as is soil that is organic, fertile, and well-drained. Plant standard or spreading sasanquas 4' to 6' apart, low-growing types 3' apart. Soak new plantings well and mulch around the plants.

Sasanquas in shade are fairly drought tolerant, but the flowers will benefit from weekly watering in late summer. Fallen petals are pretty, but rake them up and replenish mulch after flowering ends. Prune within one month to shape the plants. Fertilize in spring when new growth starts with a formula made for camellias and azaleas. While plants are young and growing actively, fertilize again in July.

Potential problems: control scale insects in early spring with oil spray.

ABOVE: 'Little Gem' magnolia (*Magnolia grandiflora* 'Little Gem')
BELOW: Holly tree (*Ilex* 'Nellie R. Stevens')

MAGNOLIA
Magnolia grandiflora 'Little Gem'
Category: sun or part shade evergreen
Use: as focal point tree for its summer flowers
Soil: organic, fertile, well-drained
Hardiness: zones 6–9
Mature size: 15' to 20' tall and 10' wide

From summer into fall, 'Little Gem' magnolia trees are dotted with fragrant small versions of the classic magnolia flower, creamy white cups of velvety petals surrounding a darker cone, and thick and shiny evergreen leaves dark green on top and brown beneath. 'Little Gem' can stand alone, a striking focal-point tree; a group of them makes an excellent windbreak screen or border backdrop.

Give 'Little Gem' sun or some shade, organic soil that drains decently, and room to grow. Ideal planting time is November through February; spring planting will only require more attention to water availability. Select the largest tree your budget allows and dig a hole twice as deep and wide as the rootball. Refill the hole with amended soil so the tree will sit at ground level, then fill in around it. Space trees 8' apart and slightly off-center in rows. Soak new trees weekly when new growth starts and keep mulched.

Fertilize magnolias each spring and again in summer to encourage new growth and flowers. Replenish mulch as it rots, working it into the soil around the trees. Prune in late winter or early spring to maintain pyramid shape and dense leaf cover.

If space allows, a traditional southern magnolia makes a bold statement in the landscape, reaching 60' tall and 30' wide at maturity. 'Edith Bogue' offers superior cold hardiness, and the more upright 'Alta' makes an especially good 30' screen.

Potential problems: few, if any, pests in well-drained soils.

HOLLY TREE
Ilex 'Nellie R. Stevens'
Category: sun or moderate shade evergreen
Use: as focal point tree for red berries in winter
Soil: fertile, well-drained
Hardiness: zones 6–9
Mature size: 20' tall

There's nothing demure about these most widely grown holly trees; they are prickly, stiffly upright in shape, and excellent at defining space and deterring intruders. Waxy leaves in several shades of green have serious spines. They blanket every branch from wide limbs at ground level to narrow pointy tops about 20' high. Small, yet notable clusters of starry white flowers appear in spring everywhere the small leaves meet the stems. Red berries mature in fall and are prized by birds as well as holiday decorators.

'Nellie R. Stevens' has a reputation for dignified performance in the garden. This holly sets the southern standard for rate of growth, naturally conical form, robust leaf cover, and bountiful berries. Others may excel in one of these qualities, but 'Nellie' has the best combination of hallmarks in one tree. Red holly hybrids, like *Ilex* x 'Oakland', come closest.

Hollies prefer an organic, fertile soil with decent drainage. Amend native soils to improve them, preparing a site in sun or shade. Cultivate an area large enough to allow the lower branches to spread gracefully to ground the tree visually. Dig a hole deeper and wider than the rootball, then refill enough to plant the holly at ground level. Water in and mulch well.

Young holly trees should be soaked deeply each week; for older trees, water less often except when berries are forming. Fertilize in early spring and again in summer to encourage new growth and maintain good green leaf color. Formulas made especially for hollies are particularly effective. Prune in early spring if needed to shape the tree.

Potential problems: if scale insects infest the tree, use an oil spray to control them.

SOUTHERN WAX MYRTLE
Myrica cerifera
Category: sun or part shade evergreen native
Use: for screens
Soil: well-drained, fertile
Hardiness: zones 7–10
Mature size: 15'

The distinctive scent of this small tree or shrub evokes its relative, bayberry, the source of holiday candles; the waxy coating on both plants is also favored by wildlife. If weather, soil, wind, or sunlight pose a challenge, southern wax myrtle meets it with confident aplomb. Gray trunks stretch out to hold up a dense, shady canopy of medium green leaves. Smaller selections are rugged and adaptable, with the same fragrant evergreen leaves.

Southern wax myrtle can be found all along our coasts, where it holds the sand and its shape in all seasons. Inland, its range extends to wet and dry soils for erosion control, large screens, and background plants for native and tropical gardens.

Prepare an area large enough to accommodate myrtle trees' habit of forming thickets. Each year, new stems will emerge from the roots to thicken the stand and can be encouraged or removed and mulched over. Dig or till the soil and amend to improve it if needed. Space young trees 3' apart or place larger specimens far enough apart so that their canopies barely overlap. Dig a hole deeper and wider than the rootball, then plant with most attractive trunks in facing view. Mulch lightly if at all.

Southern wax myrtles share the power of legumes to take nitrogen from the air around them for their nourishment. Do not overfertilize them; once yearly or less keeps a mature plant healthy without encouraging overgrowth. These myrtles tolerate extensive pruning in spring, but excess nitrogen will make more unnecessary work for you.

Potential problems: no pests.

Southern wax myrtle (*Myrica cerifera*)

BLACK GUM OR TUPELO
Nyssa sylvatica
Category: sun or partial-shade native deciduous
Use: for outstanding fall color
Soil: deep, organic, well-drained, fertile
Hardiness: zones 6–9
Mature size: 30' or more, almost as wide

Black gum, also called tupelo and sourwood, grows from a single strong trunk with an interesting, corky texture. It is native to woods' edge east of the Mississippi River. Older black gum trees reliably produce a dazzling show of yellow, orange, and finally red leaves, even in milder winters. The new leaves are wider than long and appear in spring along with lighter green flowers, which, if pollinated, yield attractive, dark blue fruit. With sharply angled branches, dark bark, and a rugged profile, black gum is as unforgettable on a gray winter day as it is in full fall color.

Any soil except consistently wet types can nurture black gum. Because the trees have only a few very thick roots, prepare an accommodating site before transplanting. Plant small trees in fall or winter, and handle the roots with care. Dig a hole twice as deep and wide as the rootball, then amend the native soil with organic matter. Refill the hole with enough of the new mix to plant the tree at ground level. Water in well and mulch lightly.

Remove any side shoots that appear in the first year to encourage one strong trunk and elevated canopy. No other pruning should be necessary unless limbs are damaged. Water regularly in well-drained soils, less often in challenging sites. Fertilize annually in spring to nurture the leaves and their colors, in fall to feed the roots.

Potential problems: no pests.

GROUND COVERS

CARPET BUGLEWEED
Ajuga reptans
Category: shade or sun perennial
Use: as low-growing lawn alternative or edging plant
Soil: organic, fertile, well-drained
Hardiness: zones 7–9
Mature size: flat clusters to 4" wide, flower spikes to 4"

So flat it is almost invisible and impervious to weeds, this hard-working ground cover shades tree and vine roots, holds soil in place, and looks great all year. At home in any well-drained soil, bugleweed is a flat mat with strong coloration in sun and a greener, looser mat in shade. Tubular flowers arise from 4"-high spikes in purple, blue, and pink shades.

ABOVE: Black gum (*Nyssa sylvatica*)
BELOW: Carpet bugleweed (*Ajuga reptans*)

Asiatic jasmine (*Trachelospermum asiaticum*)

Easy and fairly fast to grow, 'Burgundy Glow' blends white-edged green and pink leaves with blue flowers, while 'Purpurea' has delightful bronze tones among its green leaves. 'Alba' offers white flowers over green leaves, and 'Rosea' blooms pink.

This plant and its descendants will be in your garden for years to come, spreading by runners on the soil surface. Prepare the soil for planting in spring by amending it with organic matter and slow-release fertilizer. If planting under trees, do not add more than 1" of soil to the surface in one year. Instead, select small bugleweed plants and work them into soil and mulch. Water new plants well and mulch around them to control weeds.

Although carpet bugleweed will grow with almost no care, new plantings can be encouraged with regular water and fertilizer applications. As the plants cover the area, don't dig up entire clumps. Instead, transplant the smaller rosettes from around the edges for new beds and to reduce overcrowding. Use hedge shears or a string trimmer (if you're an ace) to cut down spent flower spikes.

Potential problems: few pests on healthy plants.

ASIATIC JASMINE
Trachelospermum asiaticum
Category: sun and part shade evergreen
Use: massed in beds or for effective erosion control on slopes
Soil: fertile, well-drained
Hardiness: zones 7–10
Mature size: maintain at 1' tall; spreads to 20'

Vigorous, hardy, and glossy green, the vining ground cover Asiatic jasmine strangles anything that tries to compete with it. The fine-textured vines wrap around each other endlessly to create a mat thick enough to shade out weeds. Older growth darkens and turns leathery in contrast to the brighter new growth; the effect in the garden is clean and neat. Asiatic jasmine does not bloom, but its less-hardy relative, star jasmine, does; plant a few of the fragrant stars among the Asiatic jasmines.

Till beds and amend the native soil to improve its drainage and fertility. Dig holes and space one-gallon plants 18" to 20" apart, smaller clumps a bit closer together. Water well and lay on a thick coat of pinestraw to hold weeds in check while the vines grow together. Water regularly and fertilize several times during the first season with a soluble formula.

Once the bed is established, shear annually to renew growth, thicken the stand, and control its spread. Use hedge clippers, string trimmers, or a lawn mower to reduce the jasmine's height by half. Water during dry spells to prevent wilting, and fertilize if leaves are pale in spring or summer, but not after mid-August. Without this minimal attention, some plantings become thin, but most can be rejuvenated by cutting back to near ground level.

A variegated form grows more slowly, with creamy-white patterns that offer strong contrast in shade beds, while dwarf Asiatic jasmine is particularly dense and tends to climb. 'Nortex' has narrower leaves striped with gray, giving a finer-textured appearance.

Potential problems: few pests are reported.

LILY TURF OR MONKEY GRASS
Liriope muscari or *Ophiopogon japonicus*
Category: shade or sun clumping evergreen
Use: for edging and massing in beds or shady lawn alternative
Soil: organic, well-drained
Hardiness: zones 7–9
Mature size: 8" to 12" tall and 6" to 10" wide

Lily turf and monkey grass are clumping ground covers that line paths, surround beds, and put a neat front on borders year round. Their tidy habits make everything else look better, making them essential to southern gardens.

Lily turf or liriope is generally larger than monkey grass or mondo, with wider strap leaves in a 12"-tall clump. Solid green or striped green and cream, lily turf blooms in early summer with pink, white, or violet flowers on stiff spikes. The flowers last for weeks, finally giving way to purple-black berries. Lily turf can stand more sun than monkey grass, but for a viable grass alternative in the shade, the smaller plant is unbeatable. Dark green mondo offers fine-textured, skinny leaves in dense, pincushion-like clumps.

Plant these ground covers in spring or fall. Prepare a well-drained, fertile, and organic soil for both plants to encourage their spread. Plant 8" to 10" apart, making sure not to bury the crown. Water in and mulch around the clumps with ground bark or pinestraw.

Both plants are fairly drought tolerant, but do not allow them to wilt before watering. Fertilize in early spring and again in summer as the plants are growing; to maintain a stand, fertilize once a year. Very early each spring, cut back any leaves that have become ragged. Every three years or so, cut back sharply to rejuvenate before new growth starts.

Potential problems: few, if any, pests trouble these plants.

EDIBLES

SWEET BASIL
Ocimum basilicum
Category: sun-loving annual herb
Use: spring garden annual
Soil: fertile, well-drained
Hardiness: all zones
Mature size: 6" to 24", depending on variety

You'll smell the sweetly pungent aroma of basil plants before you see or taste them. Some are very spicy and almost hot, like Thai basil, while others are lemony or recall the flavor of cloves and cinnamon. Sweet basil has smooth green leaves; other family members are purple,

ABOVE: Lily turf (*Liriope muscari*)
BELOW: Sweet basil (*Ocimum basilicum*)

Curly parsley (*Petroselinum crispum*)

wrinkled, and ruffled. These are excellent annuals to combine with other sun-lovers for texture and color contrasts. 'Spicy Globe' basil is petite, mounding, and looks great next to pom-pom zinnias in a flowerbed.

Sweet basil is the classic herb for fresh eating or cooking, especially in tomato dishes. Often planted with tomatoes, the smell of basil is said to deter insects from them. Square stem basil responds to pinching as well as coleus does, with a bonus: you can eat every pair of leaves removed to encourage the plant to branch and make more delicious leaves.

For centuries, basil has been cultivated in warm climates where at least half a day of sunshine can bring out its best aromatic oils, the source of its flavor and savoriness. Prepare well-drained, fertile soil in spring, and plant basil when you plant tomatoes. Water to prevent wilting, but not to excess. Fertilize occasionally, but avoid high levels of nitrogen that produce big, bland leaves. Keep mulched lightly. Avoid the use of pesticides on these and other food crops so you can continue picking and eating them all during the season.

Potential problems: flowers will stop leaf production, so snip them off as they appear.

PARSLEY
Petroselinum crispum
Category: sun-loving herb
Use: fall garden annual
Soil: well-drained, fertile
Hardiness: zones 7–10
Mature size: 10"

Parsley is perhaps the best example of an herb to grow over the winter in the South. You can set it out in spring, but very hot days can send it into bloom, making the leaves bitter. Start parsley, coriander, dill, and fennel as soon as plants become available locally in fall, and slip in a few cloves of garlic then, too. Even if you'll never eat parsley, grow it to nourish the larvae of swallowtail butterflies.

French curly parsley is milder to the palette, while Italian flat parsley is more flavorful and much easier to clean after harvesting. Lighter green flat parsley is a more tolerant plant in the roller-coaster conditions of southern winters. Both are good candidates for container culture, so long as the pots themselves do not freeze.

Well-drained, fertile soil will sustain parsley for many months in garden beds or pots. Mix organic matter into native dirt or potting soil and space plants 4" apart in groups. Water in well and remove any yellow leaves on young plants. Mulch lightly, just enough to suppress weeds.

Parsley, like other winter annuals, grows actively from fall through spring, and needs regular water and fertilizer. Water weekly at least in dry weather, and fertilize monthly with a complete soluble formula. When caterpillars appear, consider "rescuing" them off the plants. Take a stem or two and remove the larvae to a protected spot where they can eat to their hearts' content, pupate, and emerge as swallowtails.

Potential problems: yellowing leaves indicate a need for extra nitrogen.

ABOVE: Tomato (*Lycopersicon lycopersicum*)
BELOW: Fig tree (*Ficus* 'Brown Turkey')

TOMATO
Lycopersicon lycopersicum
Category: sun-loving annual
Use: for spring garden; fresh eating and cooking
Soil: fertile, well-drained
Hardiness: all zones
Mature size: 5' to 8' tall and 3' wide

Tomatoes are called spring vegetables, but they are technically fruits. They're called vines, but will only climb if supported. Put aside all these claims and confusions, and just grow some. Four traditional large tomato plants can easily feed two tomato lovers, while two cherry tomatoes will bear more than enough fruit to satisfy them and the neighbors. Many varieties thrive in the South, and the choices all come down to one thing: taste. Choose a variety that is locally favored, or go for the best in new offerings; but grow what your family likes (slicers, salad-size, or little jewels). A simple routine of basic care for the plants will bring out the best flavors in every kind. Nourish their needs for water, fertilizer, and space, watch out for pests, and every variety will perform for you.

Well-drained, fertile soil is essential to healthy tomatoes; consider a raised bed or 'hill' if soils are heavy, and add a sprinkling of lime to the bed. Plant tomatoes in full sun in the spring after the last frost date has passed. Space at least 2' apart and put cages or stakes in place immediately. If plants are tall, bury part of the stem. Water well, but do not mulch until soil is warm (about a month later), then maintain 1" of organic matter around the plants.

Water deeply to encourage a big root system, and often enough to prevent wilting. Fertilize at least monthly, more often if using soluble formulas. Keep "vines" and fruit off the ground.

Potential problems: usually localized and weather related; consult your neighbors or local experts for diagnosis and treatment.

FIG TREE
Ficus 'Brown Turkey', 'Black Spanish', or 'Celeste'
Category: sun-loving deciduous
Use: for fresh figs, shade
Soil: organic, fertile, well-drained
Hardiness: zones 7–10
Mature size: 8' to 15' tall and wide

Young fig trees reach 8' tall in two or three years, with leafy branches from the ground up that soon begin to put on sweet fruit and leaves up to 8" across the upper surface and equally long. Wide and tall, they compete successfully for attention with cannas, bananas, and other broad-leafed tropical plants in sunny garden beds. The trees are easy to grow and are self-pollinating.

'Brown Turkey' fig, also known as 'Black Spanish', is grown all over the South. It is relatively tidy and symmetrical in its habit, and makes a great centerpiece to the kitchen garden. The fruit is brown outside, gold and pink inside, and delicious for eating and making preserves.

Fig trees can be planted in fall or early spring. Prepare a well-drained, very organic soil in a sunny site large enough to allow the trees to reach their mature height and spread. Dig a hole twice as deep and three times as large as the rootball, then refill it with amended soil and plant the tree at ground level. Prune each stem back, water in well, and mulch deeply around the tree.

Regular watering during the growing season will result in more and sweeter fruit. Fertilize annually in early spring, but do not use large amounts of nitrogen. Prune in late winter each year as needed to keep fruit within reach.

Other fig trees to consider are 'LSU Gold' and 'LSU Purple' (bearing fruit in the school colors); 'LSU Everbearing' is a light yellow, late-season fig with excellent flavor.

Potential problems: use netting to keep birds from the fruit.

RABBIT-EYE BLUEBERRY
Vaccinium ashei 'Premier'
Category: sun-loving deciduous
Use: as hedge for excellent fall color
Soil: organic, fertile, well-drained
Hardiness: zones 7–9
Mature size: 6' to 12' tall and as wide

For garden and table, selections of the native southeastern blueberry serve both landscape and cuisine admirably. As shrubs, their small bluish-green leaves find a place in garden beds and as good companions to azalea, holly, and gardenia. Pinkish-white tiny flowers are abundant in spring; leaves turn several shades of red and gold in fall. The plants can also nourish birds and deer as part of a hedge interplanted with beautyberry and ligustrum.

Rabbit-eye blueberries are a large group of named varieties bred for southern garden conditions. Also gaining in popularity are southern high-bush blueberries. Select two or three different ones of either kind to plant together and insure good pollination. Rather than dig individual holes, dig a bed for blueberries so they can spread and thicken. Like their relatives, azaleas, blueberries must have very organic, acidic soil. Till native soil to a depth of at least 6", then add 6" of organic matter and till together. Plant blueberries 2' apart, water in well, and mulch with pinestraw.

Keep blueberries watered well from spring until the end of fruit season, then water often enough to prevent wilting. Fertilize in early spring, and add a layer of compost to the soil in spring and summer. Cut all the stems back each year after flowering until well established, then remove the oldest canes completely each year to rejuvenate the fruiting process.

Potential problems: use netting to deter birds.

Blueberry (*Vaccinium ashei*)

Preventing problems can be the key to garden success.
Keep slugs and snails away from young plants to establish sumptuous hosta beds like this one.

■ Troubleshooting in the Garden

Preventing trouble in the garden starts with smart plant choices, soil conducive to growth, and ample amounts of water and fertilizer. Add a bit of weeding and cultivating, and many common problems just never occur, especially if you work in one more practice: garden sanitation. Clean garden practices include keeping shears from spreading disease by dipping them in a 1:10 bleach in water solution between cuts to disinfect them. Good practices also extend to selecting only pest-free plants to bring into your landscape and choosing resistant and reliable varieties. Piles of lawn clippings, spent flowers, annual plants, autumn leaves, dormant perennials, and weeds do not just clutter the view. Decaying grass and weeds left strewn about become pest palaces, providing everything an infestation needs. Leaves left on the lawn all winter can reduce air circulation and keep the grass too wet, contributing to fungal infections. The same is true for browned perennials. And although they may look like sweet skirts, piles of flower petals circling the ground around a shrub quickly turn into nests for pests. Insects and diseases can find shelter in winter or summer in all that debris, so get rid of it. Simply removing weeds and taking out the debris that naturally occurs in the garden will remove the threats they harbor. You can recycle most of it by composting, but throw away badly diseased plants and troublesome weeds.

The subject of weed control gets lots of attention, but the bottom line is this: the smaller the weed plant is when you remove it, the better chance you have of keeping it out of your garden. Most people control weeds because it makes the garden look neater, without knowing the deeper reason. Each weed that you allow to remain, even though you don't want it there, takes water and nutrition away from your desirable plants. Don't let them do it, and certainly don't let them establish themselves well enough to start sending out runners underground or flinging seed all over the place. Mulch suppresses many weeds, and chemical controls make fast work of renegades where spraying is feasible. But the most effective weed control, especially around other plants, is still done by hand, while the "unwanteds" are small. Your ability to spot those small weeds, the first aphids on the roses, and baby hornworms on tomatoes makes these and many more common garden pests easier to keep in check.

WALK THE LINE

Take a walk in the garden every day, with your eyes open and perhaps a sharp hoe in hand. This is the first step of integrated pest management (IPM), a technical term for finding problems and taking care of them in the smartest ways possible. Once you've seen a change in a plant that seems troublesome (such as a leaf that doesn't unfurl or is chewed), the next step is to keep an eye on it for two reasons: to see if and how fast the problem spreads and to identify its cause. From that, decide whether the situation needs any attention from you and what action you should take. For example, if it is late August when summer annuals are attacked by insects, or midsummer when the dogwood turns red, there is no point in doing something since both are at the end of their season. But azaleas and crepe myrtles with dull leaves and misty drippings in June need solutions or their health will be lost. Smart pest control depends on your understanding of your plants, what they and you can tolerate, and what will damage them in the long run. The basic notion of IPM is that by careful observation and smart action, we can control what needs to be controlled and often do it without wholesale application of pesticides. IPM means look before you stomp, squash, or spray, and use only what is necessary to control serious pests that threaten the life of precious plants. It's cheaper for your pocketbook and means you don't have a shedful of once-used products to dispose of safely and keep away from neighborhood kids. It's also a better way of taking care of your home environment; by limiting the use of pesticides to truly serious situations, you encourage the populations of beneficial and predatory insects in the garden. And you'll feel better for that daily walk.

WHO'S WHO

Entire books are written about garden pests, their life cycles, habits, and preferred host plants. Their relationships to our favorite plants, positive or negative, should interest us as gardeners. The vast majority of critters are, if not beneficial, only a bit troublesome in large numbers. A few cannot be tolerated without losing precious flowers, tomatoes, or trees. For easy reference, group the potential pests into three categories: two-legged, four-legged, and others who have more or fewer legs. Believe it or not, humans do as much damage or more to plants, especially young ones, than any other trespasser. We often fail to take basic care of the plants or assault them with feet, lawn mowers, string trimmers, and pruning shears.

To prevent these two-legged hazards, it's a good idea to mulch around anything newly planted, especially small trees and shrubs out in the lawn. Human beings find their own traffic patterns, and the vegetation beneath them be damned. When the kids wear a path, formalize it. Forget retraining children; even if the path cuts across both lawn and flowerbed, make it permanent with steppingstones or gravel. You'll live longer. Locate beds and planting areas with mowing width in mind, both to make that task easier and prevent damage to the edging plants. Use string trimmers carefully when edging around plants; that fast-moving string can scalp the lawns' edge in one swipe, browning and dehydrating it badly. And while I do not want you to be a pruning wimp, sitting inside as the shrubs grow over the house, use caution not to cut back everything to its nubs either. Try for something between "prunophobia" (the irrational fear of pruning shears) and Edward Scissorhands. Adopt an attitude that works for you to keep plant sizes in check but enable them to achieve maturity. Sloppy, ragged cuts and untimely pruning can lead to secondary pests invading the plants; don't encourage them.

One other two-legged critter is a double-edged sword: birds. Thought of as "feathered friends" or at least great grub-eaters, birds in the garden demonstrate a dark side. Seed-eaters can devastate your backyard corn and bean patch the day after you plant it. And what an early-morning visit by a flock can do to ripe tomatoes and figs is a sin. I would be more generous if the birds ate the entire fruit, but when they simply poke their beaks in to drink a bit, I cry "Foul!" I do put out water, and net the plants, but the birds get what they like anyway. Their droppings must be cleaned off furniture and washed into the lawn below feeders and birdbaths for sanitary reasons. Still, the sight of scores of birds taking off from my back acre to darken the sky overhead warms my heart every time. Birds are pests I choose to tolerate. They do take care of the grubs in the lawn (I have never seen a mole since there's nothing for them to eat), and any insects in my trees are at great risk daily. Except occasionally, the birds earn their keep.

Four-legged pests include but are not limited to deer, dogs, cats, rabbits, squirrels, moles, voles, possums, and armadillos. Fences go a long way toward excluding them and preventing their damage, but are not always practical. Besides, hungry deer will jump right over a fence of

BACKYARD HABITAT FOR FEWER PESTS

Growing a lovely garden and one that attracts a wide variety of wildlife go hand in hand. In the natural world, for every critter there is a predator. We may not be able to get them all to come around, and will likely use at least a few nonbiological controls to reduce the damage serious pests, like fire ants, can cause. But each step taken to encourage diversity and balance in the backyard ecosystem means greater chances that nature will take its course. Many potential problems will simply seem to take care of themselves when you tend to the four principles: food, water, nest, and rest. A succession of flowers and berries in various shapes and sizes on all sorts of plants provides food for animal guests. If you are not a cat person, a birdfeeding station is a great addition. A water feature or birdbath with mist may suit your style; if not, place a pie pan of water in the lawn or set a sprinkler in a lazy arc to treat both birds and small mammals. Besides nesting boxes and trees, let a few shrubs go to form a thicket and add a bridge or rock pile to be sure there's shade and protection from wind for your visitors. With little effort over the years, we have hosted mourning doves, mockingbirds, and woodpeckers, five identifiable kinds of butterflies, lizards, garden snakes, ladybird and predator beetles, a bevy of squirrels, a rabbit family, one photogenic possum, and a 10-year resident of the rosebed, a frog known as Bumpy. Basic attention to the four principles is all it takes to get started, and before you know it, your family will be out there taking nature photographs and naming the frogs. ∎

almost any height, moles will burrow under it and cats will climb over it, and the others quite often find their way in somehow or other. There are products and home remedies said to repel all these critters; removing potential food sources is also generally suggested. Understand that repelling mammals from an area generally relies on the fact that they are intimidated by larger mammals. Nothing works universally, and most products will need to be replenished at least occasionally; but anecdotal evidence is good that most work some of the time. I have never been willing to hang bars of soap on plants to keep deer away, but I have trained cats to stay out of beds and containers by ambushing them with a water pistol. Take care when suggesting this method to young children with large, pump-up water guns; it works.

Water and kibble left outside for Rover and Fluffy not only give them an excuse to have the neighbors' pets over to party. That attractive buffet lures possums, armadillos, and rodents of all sorts to your garden. Once acclimated to your digs, they will, literally, dig you out of your lawn and flowerbeds. Mostly they're looking for grubs and other delicacies; treatments to control the pests can take you off their menu. Cats and dogs can be diggers, too, but they deserve rewards for their great ability to roust other pesky critters from the garden, including moles and voles. Just lay out their treats inside.

The third category of pests starts with slugs and snails and here the leg count ends. Those of this slimy ilk, as with deer, will go for anything they can reach, but also like deer, seem to have less taste for some silver-leafed plants. At least one gardener plagued for years by slugs planted a ring of dusty miller around all his young, tender transplants of annual flowers to deter them. If this solution doesn't suit your style, put a barrier around young, tender new growth close to the ground, such as those annuals and low-growing perennials like hosta. Try sprinkling diatomaceous earth around them or ring them with a bait containing iron phosphate. The old beer-trap method of drowning slugs was amusing, but it turns out that, like some people, slugs will come from all over the neighborhood to partake. Better are banana traps, which only seem to suit the homebodies. Prop up a short board on one end with a brick in the areas frequented by slugs and snails. In the shady space below, lay a banana peel. Come back the next morning to scoop up and throw away the peel and its new residents.

Suckers

Among the insects that commonly pester our favorite plants, there are two sorts of feasters: those with tiny mouths to pierce plants and suck their juice and those with bigger mouths to chomp and chew plant parts. The first group displays itself in various ways. Roses that open with their petals shredded and azaleas with twisted or strangely tanned leaves are teaming with thrips. You'll never see them without a hand lens, but they'll leave little brown "gifts" on the back of the leaves. If you brush a shrub and a bunch of tiny white flies buzz off, you have them. When you see sticky, cottony white stuff with hairy little bugs in it, say hello to mealybugs. If the white masses are foamy, it's spittlebugs. (Don't you love these names?) Those lumps the size of a pinhead on the new growth of tomatoes (and plenty of other plants) are aphids. Bigger lumps, usually on stems and leaves of woody plants, are scale insects whose armored coats are slick as a freshly waxed floor and just as hard to penetrate. These and other plant suckers spend their lives dehydrating plants to death.

Ever stand under a tree and feel a mist falling when it's not raining? Take a look at the other kind of damage that piercing and sucking insects can do. The mist is plant sap the insects have excreted onto the leaves below (and anything else in range), where a common airborne fungus, sooty mold, grows. Most plant viruses depend on these insects to give them a ride from plant to plant; controlling them cuts down on that dangerous traffic.

What and When to Do

Plenty of trees and shrubs can coexist successfully with a few of these insects without serious consequence. Such relationships are to be celebrated since they require no timely intervention from you. But when populations build up and damage is evident, control the insects to stop the premature leaf drop and general mess they cause. Effective measures are not always complicated. Painting mealybugs with rubbing alcohol is a time-honored practice, as is blasting aphids off roses with a strong stream of water. They're very slow to climb back up and may die in the process of returning to the buffet. Horticultural oil sprays can be very helpful in controlling them when they attack woody plants. Small trees and shrubs can be sprayed with insecticidal soap containing orange oil, azadirachtin (neem), or pyrethroids; larger trees and life-threatening infestations require a systemic insecticide such as imidacloprid for successful control. Systemic pesticides are applied to the soil around a plant and taken up through its system. When any vulnerable insect takes a bite, it's over. Note that all the control products (organic or not) are not insect-specific; to reduce collateral injury to other populations, use them only on the specific plant under attack. When using any product to control pests in the garden, read the label repeatedly, if necessary, and follow its directions and restrictions carefully to maximize its effect and minimize potential risks.

Chompers

The second major category of insect pests contains the chewers, including caterpillars, cutworms, beetles, grasshoppers, and many others. Fortunately, their damage is less discreet and often evident sooner in their life cycle. In fact, some of them are the larvae of beloved butterflies and moths, so it is important to recognize damage you can live with for the magnificent result. Caterpillars devouring dill are likely swallowtails, but the ones defoliating tomatoes definitely aren't and must be controlled to save the BLTs. Offenders can be plucked off the plants and dropped into a bucket of soapy water. For more fun perhaps, five-year-old children love to stomp and squash, and it gives you the chance to teach them to differentiate between good and bad bugs, especially if they've had an encounter with one of the famous stinging caterpillars that swarm down from trees.

Some chewers have devious ways of protecting themselves from you and their natural predators. Leaf rollers are a particular problem for canna lilies, evidenced by leaves and flowers that never unfurl; webworms spin large, ugly webs in trees. Physical controls work wonders against these pests: cut down the canna stalks that are damaged. Then wrap a broom in cheesecloth to sweep the webs away. Remove all that material from the garden immediately.

Many big-mouthed beetles chew neat holes in leaves and flowers all night long, then often retreat to a stupor in the morning. Lay a sheet under the affected plant early enough and a simple rustle of the leaves will release dozens of the sleepy beetles onto the cloth for easy disposal. The exception is the tiny flea beetle, named for its size and hopping habit. Grasshoppers and their friends the locusts are usually a short-term problem, making control impractical since they're gone by the time you notice they've been there. The products useful in controlling chewing insects range from diatomaceous earth to rotenone. You can also use natural predators (e.g., milky spore and *Bacillus thuriengensis,* known as dipel or thuricide). In general, the predators are slower to get a grip on the situation and thus should be used when the first few insects are spotted. Reserve the others for rare situations where sanitation and the predators fail, leading to population explosions of resistant scoundrels. Use controls only on plants with problems; random application doesn't solve the real problem and causes others.

A few other "bugs" often become pests, including spider mites (actually arachnids) and leaf miners (the larvae of some moths, beetles, and flies). Mites thrive in hot, dry conditions and their damage starts with tiny flecks of yellow on leaves that you may not notice. Soon the leaves look bronzed on their way to turning brown, potentially causing the death of the branch or entire plant. Regular watering, including a good spray with the hose in dry weather, keeps the leaves clean and makes conditions less favorable for spider mites. If you suspect browned junipers or dull-looking lantana has spider mites, try this test. Hold a piece of white paper under the suspect branch and shake it. If the dust that falls off moves or is red, say "Eureka!", because

At first glance, the praying mantis may be hard to see. Its natural camouflage is designed to fool the insects it eats daily by allowing the mantis to blend in with surrounding plants.

you've found them. If pruning out the damage fails, use a horticultural oil spray (not dormant oil unless it's wintertime) or a product containing neem to break up the mites.

Leaf miners do what their name suggests: the larvae eat their way through the leaves, tunnelling (or mining) in every direction. A green leaf looks like a roadmap to nowhere has been drawn on it with white lines. Because leaf miners are inside the leaves, sprays and dusts do not reach them. Remove damaged leaves on azalea, coral honeysuckle, and other perennials, then spray the new growth with a product containing neem to slow down the egg-laying mothers. Woody plants with serious infestations can require heavy pruning or systemic insecticides to control the pests. If miners (or other insects with similar habits like squash-vine borers) become a problem in vegetables or herbs, you can exclude them with floating row covers. These white fabric sheets let in light and water but keep out flying insects that can lay eggs on vegetable and flower transplants. Handy, inexpensive, effective, and easy to store, row covers are a great option for butterfly-host plants, too. If you want parsley, but want the butterfly larvae to have their fill, too, cover some of the plants so eggs aren't laid on the ones you plan to eat.

Pesky Pathogens

As if insect pests weren't enough, pathogens will try for a foothold in your garden, but you can prevent many of both with the same gardening practices. A clean garden, a daily walk-through, and growing conditions that contribute to plant health will go far. Three kinds of rascals make up this posse: fungi, bacteria, and viruses. With any luck, you'll never encounter any of them. When you do, here's what you can expect.

As indicated, viral diseases have to get to your plants via an infected host. Insects, pollens, seeds, plant parts used in propagation, and even your own hands can spread a virus, but avoidance of this problem is relatively easy. Once a plant gets a virus, it should be physically removed from the garden, a practice called "roguing out." To control the insects from the beginning, purchase certified seed and store any seed you save away from heat, disinfect pruning tools, and wear gloves or keep your hands clean to prevent virus infections.

Bacterial diseases often depend on humid, rainy weather to get going in your plants, but are deposited there by the same suspects as the transporters of viruses, so the same practices work to deter them in most cases. A most unfortunate example of bacteria is fireblight, a serious problem when encountered in Bradford pears, firethorns, and related plants. Entire branches or limbs leaf out in spring, then wilt, turn red, and finally look burned, all thanks to bacteria using the plant as their food source. Removal, heavy pruning, and preventive spraying the following year are all options for combatting fireblight. Many bacteria are known as secondary invaders, opportunistic devils who take advantage of any opening in plant surfaces to move right in and start multiplying. Remove damaged fruit from the garden and keep tools clean and use them carefully to avoid wounding plants and creating opportunities for bacteria to invade.

Fungus Gangs

Fungi are particularly pernicious, because they are not as easily avoided as viral and bacterial invaders. When you consider that they make billions of spores, each capable of infection, and that they are the ultimate hitchhikers, it is amazing that our environment is not overrun with fungus disease. Wind, water, insects, equipment, and people can move fungi around effectively; fingi can survive off their host for the time it takes to get there. And "there" is everywhere for fungi; some, but not all, are fatal to plants. More, however, merely ruin a plant's good looks and your happiness, so it's good to know a bit about them. First understand that by the time you see any damage from fungus, there's little you can do at that moment to alleviate the problem immediately. Fungus diseases like black spot on roses and brown patch in St. Augustine grass have killed the leaves and blades that you see, but the rest of the plant is still alive and can be readily regrown. Prevent the next outbreak of fungus by applying fungicide as the next new growth emerges. Unlike insecticides, fungicides alter the basic conditions on the plants to make them inhospitable to the spores.

Clues to Use

Wilting is a symptom you might notice on many plants, and most gardeners' first impulse is to water immediately. If the plant is still wilted the next day, you water again, and so forth, until you realize something else is going on. That something else can be chronic overwatering (by you or Mother Nature) or soggy roots, which happens when soils are not well-drained enough for the plants. By fixing the drainage or moving the plant to a shadier location if that seems appropriate, the plant can recover readily. But worse yet, there may be root rot fungi attacking the plant. Sad to say, root rot fungi swim in the soil solution, so once a plant in a row gets it, the others may show decline one after another. The progress of this fungi is depressing to watch and usually fatal. Some plants have inbred resistance to root rot and others are grafted to avoid it; good drainage and watering sensibly prevent it.

Leaf spots may be no problem at all, or may indicate an ongoing issue that needs attention. Hedges of red-top (*Photinia glabra*) display brilliant red new growth each spring, but many older ones are plagued by leaf spot. Replacement is an option, as is frequent pruning to remove the damage. The good news is that all that pruning on top keeps the hedge thick, since spraying enough and effectively is impractical. Black spot can also be pruned away on many rose varieties; spraying the new growth with fungicide may help prevent reinfection if the weather cooperates with dry, sunny days. Both these fungus diseases occur repeatedly, and gardeners can find themselves spraying with fungicide almost weekly but still seeing the symptoms. If replacing the plants is not an option, rotate fungicides. Buy two different products suitable for your plants, and use first one and then the other to confuse the fungi.

Oddballs to Know

Just when you think you've got the hang of these pathogens—that they thrive in moist, wet conditions and can be kept at bay by controlling insects and keeping the garden clean—there's a curve ball named powdery mildew. This fungus is abundant in humid air, but its spores need dry leaf surfaces to get started. Come to think of it, that's just how southern weather cycles go very often, from dry days to increased humidity to a thunderstorm and back to dry. White or gray patches appear on the leaves, then every plant part can be affected. The cycle of powdery

LET 'EM BE!

A wonderful gardener told me that there are not good and bad bugs, except from our point of view. I agreed, but resisted her efforts to rename them good and better bugs. We do agree that too many beneficial critters (ones who can lunch on other bugs we'd like to be rid of) are almost unrecognizable to most gardeners and the roles of others are misunderstood. Get to know these friendly and desirable garden predators. This happy group begins with frogs, lizards, toads, spiders, and sometimes birds. Lacewings look like their name, small green bugs with lacy wings, and their babies strangely resemble tiny alligators and will eat their weight in aphids and other pests. True bugs include intriguingly named damsels and assassins. The ladies are 1/2" long, gray or brown with long pointy beaks with which to poke their prey, including small caterpillars and aphids. Adults have wings and are easier to spot than the nymphs, but both eat plenty. Meet the beetles: ladybirds (you know them as ladybugs and not all of them are red), ground beetles, soldiers, and minute pirates, also called flower bugs. Ground beetles, usually about 1" long, sport a shiny black shell and jointed and prominent legs, all of which give it an advantage over other insects, even snails and slugs or at least their eggs. Soldier beetles have leathery jackets in various hues, and are skinny with long antennae and heads that are often differently colored. They'll snack on any critter with a soft body that they can find. Truly tiny, flower bugs are no more than 1/8" long but can do some real munching on tiny thrips and spider mites. Tachinid flies look sort of like houseflies, but are gray. Their larvae are green. Syrphid flies won't sting you, but will fool you into thinking they are bees, but they have only one set of wings and produce dozens of fanged larvae that love to eat aphids. Most of these beneficial insects commonly appear in gardens and you can purchase others to release. Since most of the adults feed on larvae and pollen, growing a diverse variety of flowering plants and limiting the use of pesticides in the garden will encourage them mightily.■

mildew has such an impact on crepe myrtle, it is one of the diseases the new varieties are bred to resist. Plant them and avoid the nasty business entirely or plan to spray when the disease occurs.

Two additional common problems may confront and confound you because they don't look like the others. Sometimes azaleas or gardenias will develop yellowing between the veins of their leaves. This condition is called "chlorosis" and happens when the plant cannot get enough iron from the soil. You can add iron to the soil, spray the plant, or simply incorporate more organic matter to change the soil chemistry. Plants that look sunburned often actually are. Leaf surfaces develop irregular patches of sheen and may turn bronze; branches can split and flowers and fruit are ruined. Avoid moving plants from shade into sun without a transition time to let them get used to the extra rays, whether they are houseplants moving out for the summer or new shrubs kept in shade at the nursery but intended for sunny gardens.

Dangerous Invaders

Invasive plants are the felons of the garden world. Gardeners have become victims of our own excess as we have scoured the world for more and better plants. Such foreigners were welcomed into our society, representing themselves as generous ambassadors from other countries, each a paragon of virtue for beautiful flowers or dynamic form. In truth, many are noxious weeds, plants growing where they have no business. These bullies are not merely rampant reseeders that are easily dealt with by pulling or spraying. Truly invasive plants crowd out other species and resist your efforts to remove or even control them. When the worst invaders take over a plot of ground, native plants and the wildlife that depends on them are threatened and too often lost. Each state has an invasive plants council that distributes information about noxious plants damaging to local plants, but the top of my personal list is little-leaf privet. With soft green, small leaves, these shrubs and small trees that spread both by runners and by seed have taken over in many places, shading out everything that used to grow at ground level in the southern environment. Check your area for a "privet pull" or other community project to reduce and remove invasive plants, and don't add them to your garden.

CONTROL FREAKS, REJOICE

Ultimately troubleshooting using smart gardening practices is all about exerting your control on the garden to keep its contents in check and suit your garden style. If that sounds daunting, remember that although the world is out of your control, there is always the garden. You can move plants to give them a new start, prune them hard or not, or change fertilizers to see what happens. The decision to control serious pests or replace the plants is yours entirely. War won't break out either way. When you prevent most troubles and control only the particularly harmful pests, the garden benefits and so do you. The gain comes in more and prettier flowers, dragonflies hovering over a nicer lawn to lay on, and less routine maintenance to detract from pure garden enjoyment time with friends and family.

Resources

In using these resources, you will be introduced to the vast world of gardening advice, tips, and ideas. Reliable sources beyond this list include local events like flower and garden shows, gardening programs at botanic gardens and libraries, and local gardening columnists and media types. Ask questions where you shop for plants and supplies. Make friends with the horticulturist at your nearby garden center, a local landscape architect, any master gardener you meet, and the county extension agent in your area. Don't forget to grill your mama and the other gardeners in your family and in your neighborhood. Just write down what they tell you, so when you pass it on to someone else, they'll get the same good advice you did.

SEEDS, PLANTS, AND OTHER GARDEN PRODUCTS

When shopping for garden "stuff," always start local. Visit all the garden centers within driving distance at least once, and get to know the horticulturist at a nearby nursery. Often the locals know which particular variety of a plant will grow best for you and what soil amendments are most affordable. For good customers, they can also order many items not on their shelves.

There is also a world of nurseries across our region and beyond. Some you can visit in person, some are set up well for shopping on-line, and most have catalogs to tempt and woo you. An asterisk (*) after the name indicates the nursery includes a shop and/or gardens you can visit.

Plants

Niche Gardens*
1111 Dawson Rd.
Chapel Hill, NC 27516
919-967-0078
www.nichegardens.com

Wayside Gardens
1 Garden Lane
Hodges, SC 29695-0001
800-213-0379
www.waysidegardens.com

Stokes Tropicals*
4806 E. Old Spanish Trail (Hwy. 182,
  between New Iberia and Jeanerette)
Jeanerette, LA 70544
337-365-6998
www.stokestropicals.com
Bananas, cannas, and many more
tropicals

Antique Rose Emporium
9300 Lueckmeyer Rd.
Brenham, TX 77833
800-441-0002
www.wearoses.com

Steve Ray's Bamboo Gardens*
250 Cedar Cliff Rd.
Springville, AL 35146
205-594-3438
www.thebamboogardens.com

Cala's Tropicals
2209 Clinton Hwy.
Powell, TN 37849
865-945-5584
www.calastropicals.com

Gardener's Supply Company
128 Intervale Rd.
Burlington, VT 05401
888-833-1412
www.gardeners.com
Wide range of supplies, including indoor-light gardening

Gardens Alive!
5100 Schenley Pl.
Lawrenceburg, IN 47025
513-354-1483
www.gardensalive.com
Alternative pest control, including good diagnostic information

Vegetable and Flower Seeds

Park Seed Company*
1 Parkton Ave.
Greenwood, SC 29647
800-213-0076
www.parkseed.com
Full line of seeds and supplies

Johnny's Selected Seeds
955 Benton Ave.
Winslow, ME 04901
800-879-2258
www.johnnyseeds.com
Specialty vegetables and flowers, including short-season choices

Tomato Growers Supply Co.
P.O. Box 60015
Fort Meyers, FL 33906
888-478-7333
www.tomatogrowers.com
More than 500 varieties of tomatoes and peppers

Willhite Seed, Inc.
P.O. Box 23
Poolville, TX 76487-0023
800-828-1840
www.willhiteseed.com
Wide selection of heat-tolerant vegetables

Renee's Garden
7389 W. Zayante Rd.
Felton, CA 95018
888-880-7228
www.reneesgarden.com
Superior seeds and unique collections

Bulbs

Brent and Becky's Bulbs*
7900 Daffodil Lane
Gloucester, VA 23061
804-693-3966
www.brentandbeckysbulbs.com
Huge selection of daffodils and more

**Old House Gardens—
Heirloom Bulbs**
536 Third St.
Ann Arbor, MI 48103
734-995-1486
www.oldhousegardens.com
Extensive collection of southern heirloom plants

Louisiana Nursery*
1908 Parkview Dr.
Opelousas, LA 70570
337-948-3696
www.durionursery.com
Louisiana iris and other southern favorites

WEB SITES

www.gardenmama.com. *Nellie (A.K.A. "Garden Mama") Neal's web site, with thousands of questions from real gardeners answered on site, tips, features, articles, and shopping.*

www.garden.org. *The National Gardening Association offers tons of general gardening information, shopping, and bimonthly columns that are very specific. Our part of the country is divided into three regions, so you can find out what to do where you live.*

www.griffin.peachtree.edu/bae. *This type of site is very valuable for understanding local weather conditions. Georgia gardeners will find it helpful, while the rest of us search for similar sites in our states.*

www.gardentimeonline.com/SouthCarolina.html. *A compendium links to 1,200 gardening sites in the main site, with pages like this one tailored to South Carolina gardeners.*

www.ces.ncsu.edu/depts/hort/consumer. *"Hort on the Internet" at North Carolina State University includes plants, garden topics, and quick reference information.*

http://www.victoryseeds.com/information/regional/al.html. *Handy links to the Alabama Cooperative Extension Service on-line, among other links of interest to gardeners.*

www.gardenweb.com/forums/tngard. *For gardeners in Tennessee who want to correspond with other gardeners in their state, this forum is part of the huge GardenWeb site, where gardeners swap information, pictures, and plant lore.*

www.mississippigardener.com. *From the magazine of the same name, the site features forums, a calendar of events, and contacts at the magazine for asking garden questions.*

www.louisianalawnandgarden.org. *Links to LSU's Cooperative Extension Service, with information, articles, and a calendar of gardening events.*

www.gardening.cornell.edu. *Cornell University's site for home gardeners is a treasure trove of information, some of it suitable for gardeners in our region.*

www.thegardenhelper.com. *A site for beginners, with good basic information. Not tailored to our region, but discusses universal garden principles.*

www.kidsgardening.com. *Bookmark this one and give it to the P.T.S.A. and your kids' teachers. It's an award-winner and suggests lots of ways to get kids involved in gardening, without letting them know it's educational, too.*

www.growinglifestyle.com/us/h208. *Articles at the University of Arkansas about home gardening, with links to more sites and information for gardeners.*

COOPERATIVE EXTENSION SERVICE

Contact the county agent or horticulturist in your county (or parish) about educational programs and gardening information, and to contact the master gardeners in your area. Use these links to locate the cooperative extension service nearest you; their current phone numbers are listed in the government section of your local directory.

Alabama: www.aces.edu

Arkansas: www.uaex.edu

Georgia: www.ces.uga.edu

Louisiana: www.lsuagcenter.com/nav/extension/

Mississippi: www.msucares.com

North Carolina: www.ces.ncsu.edu

Oklahoma: www1.dasnr.okstate.edu/oces

South Carolina: www.clemson.edu/extension

Tennessee: www.tnstate.edu/cep/

SUGGESTED READING

Aronovitz, Avis Y., *Gardening 'Round Atlanta* (Eldorado Publishers, 1996).
Tips you won't find anywhere else, with very specific information about "Hotlanta" gardens.

Bender, Steve, ed., *The Southern Living Garden Book* (Oxmoor House, 1998).
The only encyclopedia of southern plants that meets the definition. If you want a look at the scope of our region's flora, this book belongs on your shelf.

Chaplin, Lois Trigg, *The Southern Gardener's Book of Lists: The Best Plants for All Your Needs, Wants, and Whims* (Taylor Trade Publishing, 1994).
An astounding collection of plant choices for every situation imaginable.

Dirr, Michael A., *Dirr's Trees and Shrubs for Warm Climates: An Illustrated Encyclopedia* (Timber Press, 2002).
Start in Dr. Dirr's personal garden and you'll follow him everywhere to learn about the plants you're growing and the ones you'll want to grow.

Grissell, Eric, *Insects and Gardens: In Pursuit of a Garden Ecology* (Timber Press, 2001).
The best volume about what bugs are actually up to in your garden.

Hill, Madalene, and Gwen Barclay, with Jean Hardy, *Southern Herb Growing* (Shearer Publishing, 1987).
On its way to being a classic in gardening writing. This mother-daughter team expands your definition of "herbs" to include perennials you love to grow, but didn't know anything about.

Neal, Nellie. *Questions and Answers for Deep South Gardeners* (BB Mackey Books, 2002).
Based on the author's radio show, this is a problem-solving primer for gardeners.

Pleasant, Barbara, *Warm-Climate Gardening: Tips, Techniques, Plans, Projects for Humid or Dry Conditions* (Garden Way Books, Storey Communications, 1993).
This book fills a big void in southern gardening information. Very practical and useful.

Pope, Thomas, Neil Odenwald, and Charles Fryling Jr., *Attracting Birds to Southern Gardens* (Taylor Trade Publishing, 1993).
A must-have book for those planting habitat to attract migratory birds and songbirds.

Seidenberg, Charlotte, *The New Orleans Garden* (University Press of Mississippi, 1993).
Unequaled for its historic perspective as well as its plant growing info.

Shoup, G. Michael, *Roses in the Southern Garden* (Antique Rose Emporium, 2000).
An excellent reference book for antique roses, and a fine source for buying them as well.

Sullivan, Barbara J., *Garden Perennials for the Coastal South* (University of North Carolina Press, 2003).
This book includes the plants best suited to our coastal region and is written in a friendly style that will inspire you to try them.

Wilson, Jim, *Jim Wilson's Container Gardening* (Taylor Trade Publishing, 2000).
If you don't already garden in containers, you will, and this book tells you all you need to know. In fact, anything written by Jim Wilson is worth reading, so seek him out.

Winter, Norman, *Tough-as-Nails Flowers for the South* (University Press of Mississippi, 2003).
More than 150 proven performers for southern gardens.

Index

NOTE: page numbers in italics indicate illustrations.

Index

Index